EDITION 2

Today's
CHRISTIAN
HERETICS?

ED HOURY

dba ALTRUITY PUBLICATIONS LLC

Today's Christian Heretics? Edition 2

ISBN-13: 978-1-7348455-2-5 (Paperback)
ISBN-13: 978-1-7348455-3-2 (Ebook)

Library of Congress Control Number: 2021906486

All biblical references are from the New Revised Standard Version, Copyrighted in 1989 and published by Thomas Nelson, Inc., Nashville, Tennessee 37214. All Rights Reserved.

Designed by Debbi Stocco
Cover photo credit: ID 106991303 © Matthew Bamberg | Dreamstime.com

TABLE OF CONTENTS

PREFACE

A Gallup poll showed that in 2020 the number of Americans who belonged to a church, synagogue, or mosque fell to 47 percent, the lowest percentage since these records were kept in 1937. Organized religion, especially Christianity which accounted for the largest drop in numbers, has seen a steady decline in membership. Sadly, Christianity long ago left its moorings and is losing its relevance in today's world.

Jesus delivered a universal, humanistic message which has been lost by today's Christianity. He emphasized loving our neighbors as ourselves, living by the golden rule, being magnanimous to those who ask of us, caring for the poor, the afflicted, and the imprisoned by acting and giving, not just remuneration from our abundance, but giving time, effort and love, with self-sacrifice to those from whom no love, return or remuneration is sought, quietly and without notoriety.

These requirements have been relegated to near obscurity and insignificance by the Nicene form of Christianity developed by the Greco-Roman influenced church in Rome, centuries after Jesus ministry, and later by the Reformation that abolished the need for faith-based works. Nevertheless, it is the Nicene form of Christianity that is preached in today's churches, and practiced by Jesus' alleged followers. This has resulted in our downward spiral of greed and undue influence corrupting our democracy, worsening our confiscatory concentration of wealth, exploiting our large majority, and increasing our national debt.

Jesus instructed that *"Not everyone who says to me 'Lord, Lord' will enter the kingdom of heaven, but only the one who does the will of my Father in heaven"* (Matthew 7:21-23, and similarly Mark 3:35, Luke 6:46, James 1:22, 1 John 2:17, Romans 2:13). Who is doing the will of the Father in today's world? Who are today's Christian heretics? This book was written to raise these questions and the awareness levels of who is doing the will of the Father in today's world, to open minds and hearts, and to promote a better understanding of what Jesus' teachings mean for followers of Jesus in today's world.

Today, there are 7.8 billion persons on this earth, 7.6 billion more than in Jesus' day. In Jesus' day the earth was considered to be flat and the center of the universe. Today we have landed humans on the moon and robots on Mars. Today, we understand the falsehoods of the Roman and Greek pantheon of gods and goddesses, though they were revered by their people. Today's world is a very different world than Jesus' world of 2,000 years ago, and we are a very different people. Nevertheless, today's churches and seminaries continue to promote a form of Christianity that has little to do with Jesus' ministry, or to adapt Jesus' ministry to today's world.

Historically, Nicene Christianity was developed during the first five-centuries in the Church of Rome under the auspices of the Roman Empire. It replaced the pantheon of Greek and Roman gods and goddesses. In the first few centuries of the Common Era (CE) even Roman emperors were recognized and considered as gods. Julius Caesar, his son Augustus, Emperor Antoninus Pius and his wife Faustina are just a few examples. Given the Roman and Greek proclivity for beliefs in multiple gods and goddesses at the time, their interests in diffusing the oneness of the Judaic God by including first Jesus, and then the Holy Spirit to form a Holy Trinity as God, might be understandable. The Romans and Greeks were the Gentiles of their time. They controlled the Church in Rome and its developing belief system. In the context of believing in a flat earth being the center of the universe, and in their pantheon of gods and goddesses, their interests included developing Christian beliefs and distinguishing them from Judaic beliefs.

Recognition of the Roman and Greek influence on the development of Christianity after Jesus' ministry is nothing new. President, Thomas Jefferson, a prodigious intellect of his day, recognized this fact more than two centuries ago in writing about Jesus to a friend. See Chapter 1, THE BIBLE: HISTORICAL CONTEXT: INERRANCY, Subchapter, The Jefferson Bible, where Jefferson stated:

> [Jesus' teachings] have been still more disfigured by the corruptions of schematizing followers, who have found an interest in sophisticating and perverting the simple doctrine he taught, by engrafting on them the mysticisms of a Grecian Sophist (Plato), frittering them into subtitles and obscuring them with jargon, until they have caused good men to reject the whole in disgust, and to view Jesus as an imposter…

> I am a disciple of the doctrines of Jesus, very different from the Platonists…who draw all their characteristic dogmas from what its author never said nor saw. They have compounded from the heathen mysteries a system beyond the comprehension of man of which [Jesus], were he to return to earth, would not recognize one feature.

Rather than advocating and promoting Jesus' teachings, today's churches promote the Nicene form of Christianity and the preaching of the Apostle Paul. Paul defined being a Christian and achieving salvation in terms of accepting Jesus as our Lord and Savior, because Jesus allegedly died for our sins. We are all allegedly afflicted with original sin, even at birth, because of Genesis' portrayal of Adam's alleged original sin of eating the forbidden fruit.

The concept of original sin permeating all future generations was unknown to Jesus and his disciples and didn't originate with them. The concept originated with the Apostle Paul, though he didn't use that term. These issues are treated in Chapter 2, THE APOSTLE PAUL AND ACTS, Chapter 3, ORIGINAL SIN, and Chapter 4, THE HISTORICAL CONTEXT OF THE GOSPEL OF JOHN. The Original Sin theory wasn't fully developed until the writings of St. Augustine in the late 4th century.

Though Paul and others were successful in extending knowledge of Jesus' crucifixion and resurrection among the Gentiles, unfortunately, much of Jesus' ministry and message was lost in the process. Christianity became much more a religion about Jesus himself, rather than about Jesus' religion and ministry on behalf of God. God didn't appoint or send Jesus to be worshipped. God sent Jesus to teach humanity to live in accordance with God's examples and teachings. We are not doing so.

Jesus' message didn't include promoting himself as our Lord and Savior. Rather, Jesus preached that salvation could only be achieved by doing the will of the Father. It was Paul who preached that Gentiles and Jews can achieve everlasting life by simply accepting Jesus as their Lord and Savior. Jesus never said so. Paul was not a disciple of Jesus. Paul never met Jesus except in a vision. Paul seldom referred to Jesus' teachings. Paul already believed in a resurrection and an afterlife as a Pharisee, even before Jesus' resurrection.

Paul's conversion experience was not unlike that of Joseph Smith Jr. Like Paul, Smith was not a disciple of Jesus. However, he saw visions of Jesus and God, and was led to a book of buried golden plates by an angel. Smith wrote the Book of Mormon that led to the founding of the Mormon Church. These issues are discussed in Chapter 2, THE APOSTLE PAUL AND ACTS. Jesus' ministry and teachings are discussed in Chapters 6, WHAT WERE JESUS' TEACHINGS?, and in chapter 7, THE LORD'S PRAYER.

Webster's defines a *heretic* as "*a dissenter from established church dogma*". In the 4th century, those who believed that Jesus was God were led by Athanasius of Alexandria. Arius of Alexandria and his followers believed that Jesus did not always exist, as did God. The controversy led to the Council of Nicaea in 325 CE, convened at the behest of Roman Emperor, Constantine I. Though Constantine had converted to Christianity after belief in the Roman Pantheon of gods and goddesses, he refused to be baptized until he was on his death bed to insure his entry to heaven. In any event, settling the Arian controversy would assist in Constantine's task of governing.

Though the question of whether Jesus is God is most likely not within the human province to definitively know, particularly some three hundred years after Jesus' ministry, the fallible Nicaea Council members, concerned they would disappoint the Emperor by failing to reach a conclusion, nevertheless decided that Jesus was God. Many of the churches in the eastern parts of the Roman Empire based in Constantinople continued in their Arian beliefs.

Eventually, Roman Emperor Theodosius I convened a second church council in 381 CE that confirmed the Nicene beliefs. This Council also added the Holy Spirit to the concept of God. Its conclusions were not confirmed as ecumenical until 451 CE at the Council of Chalcedon. Thus, largely due to the influence of Roman emperor governance and politics, the concept of the Holy Trinity that included Jesus and the Holy Spirit as God didn't become *established church dogma until the fifth century.*

To this day Roman Catholics and the Eastern Orthodox differ as to the origin of the Holy Spirit. This is the so called filioque issue, relating to whether the Holy Spirit originates only from God, or from God and Jesus. Like today's Christianity, today's Bible was essentially imposed on the Christian world by the Church in Rome at the end of the 4th century under the auspices of the Roman Empire. (See Chapter 1, THE BIBLE: HISTORICAL CONTEXT: INERRANCY.)

After the fifth century, Christian beliefs remained relatively unchanged for 1,000 years until the 16th century Protestant Reformation initiated by Martin Luther. The Reformation was brought about largely as a reaction to the corrupt practices of the Church of Rome involving the sale of indulgences by the church to the wealthy to guarantee their salvation. Faith-based works as a basis for salvation had been fundamental Christian dogma for 1,500 years. Rather than considering the sale of indulgences as an aberration and not faith-based works, Martin Luther abolished the need for faith-based works, for the concept of justification by faith alone.

The Eastern Orthodox churches never developed the corrupt practice of selling indulgences, and were totally unaffected by the Reformation. We now have salvation based on individuals' assessments of their faith in accepting Jesus as their Lord and Savior. Faith-based works still has a place in the theology of the Roman Catholic and Eastern Orthodox churches, though faith-based works cannot guarantee salvation. (See Chapter 5, THE REFORMATION: JUSTIFICATION BY FAITH ALONE: PREDESTINATION.)

Christians in the United States have historically comprised virtually all the presidents, the overwhelming majority of the members of Congress, the overwhelming number of the 50 governors, the overwhelming majority of the members of the 50 state legislatures, state and federal judges, and the majority of Supreme Court justices. This nation is essentially headed where its Christian leadership is taking it.

Rather than being inculcated with Jesus' ministry, it appears we are headed into a worsening downward spiral of greed and undue influence corrupting our democracy, worsening our confiscatory concentration of wealth, exploiting our large majority, and increasing our national debt. (See Chapters 9 through 19.)

As stated above, today's world is a far different world than Jesus' world, and we are a far different people. With globalization, mass communications and airline travel, our neighbors today are not simply the Samaritans of Jesus' day; people we personally encounter essentially living in the next zip code or county. Like the people in Wuhan, China, where the Covid-19 virus originated, and the actions of the Chinese government, the actions of the government we elect and pay taxes to support directly affect many persons locally, our state, across our country, and the world. We need to better adapt Jesus' teachings to today's world. We need to better understand the implications, impacts and repercussions of our political activities in light of Jesus' teachings. (See Chapter 8, CHURCHES TODAY: PROMOTING SALVATION?)

The failure to emphasize the values and obligations Jesus preached, rather than simply accepting Jesus as Lord and Savior, has had serious adverse social and political consequences. Much of what is happening to our nation in terms of the degradation and corruption of our democracy, the confiscatory concentration of wealth, the exploitation of the large majority, can be traced to the fact that the Christianity practiced by many of today's churches and Christian persons ignores the behaviors and obligations imposed by Jesus' ministry. Even our justice system and many of our universities have been corrupted and are conveying propaganda laced information favoring influential interests exercising undue influence. (See Chapter 9, ORIGINALISM: UNDERMINING DEMOCRAY?, and Chapter 10, UNDUE INFLUENCE: THE CONCENTRATION OF WEALTH.)

Today, we now have a well-funded and expanding Christian-influenced, Federalist Society espousing originalist interpretation of the Constitution that was never advocated by the founding fathers. Because of British corporations' exploitation of the Colonists, the founding fathers held corporations in suspicion and limited their endeavors. Corporations never had free speech or religious rights. Corporations are not citizens of our society. Corporations cannot vote or hold office. Their controlling interests could be in the hands of non-citizens whose interest conflict with the interests of voters.

Nevertheless, our Christian influenced, Federalist Society controlled Supreme Court has granted corporations free speech and religious rights, while degrading the constitutional and human rights of individuals. In Citizens United v. Federal Election Commission (2010), the Federalist Society influenced Supreme Court found that the bipartisan McCain–Feingold Campaign Finance Reform Act was unconstitutional, because the Act's political campaign spending limits violated the free speech of corporations and anonymous donors. Though bribing one politician for a single bill used to be illegal, it's now legal for corporations and anonymous donors to spend unlimited millions to get politicians elected so that politicians are beholden to their donors' best interests during their entire term of office.

The Supreme Court exploited the powerless majority by ruling that arbitration agreements can be imposed as a condition of employment on workers and job applicants, supplanting the constitutional right to a trial by jury and the statutory right of concerted action, Epic Systems v Lewis (2018). In deciding individual workers can contract away their rights, though dealing with the disparate power of multi-million dollar corporations, the court gutted the constitutional right of workers to jury trials, and the statutory right of concerted action guaranteed under the National Labor Relations Act. There is no establishing justice, promoting the general welfare, and securing the blessings of liberty for the people as required by the Preamble to the Constitution, except for corporations and the wealthy exercising undue influence. These issues are discussed in Chapter 9, ORIGINALISM: UNDERMINING DEMOCRACY?

Though large corporations, businesses and wealthy individuals are essential for the creation of jobs and the promotion of commerce, our democracy is increasingly dominated and governed by a wealthy and influential cabal exercising undue influence through lobby groups, foundations, non-profits, anonymous entities and think tanks that manipulate our captive politicians to the detriment of the large majority. In serving the undue influence many of our politicians have allowed the neglect of the environment, exacerbated the concentration of wealth, and accelerated the drift towards a corrupted democracy in exchange for re-election support, opportunities for enrichment, cushy trips and comfortable landings for themselves and their families when they retire. These issues are treated in more detail in Chapter 10, UNDUE INFLUENCE: THE CONCENTRATION OF WEALTH.

The Kiplinger Letter of July 2019 reported that this shadow economy is actually a massive, unregulated, $15 trillion industry that makes up about 70% of the size of the entire United States economy. The 2016 Panama Papers revealed how persons in the shadow economy obscure their wealth and exploitation through off-shore shell corporations and tax havens. The wealthy and influential have legions of well-paid lobbyists, think tanks, private foundations, non-profit organizations, anonymous groups and indebted politicians in their hire. Until the Covid-19 pandemic we had the lowest unemployment in decades, with record high stock market indices and corporate profitability, yet wages for workers were stagnant. Though this shadow economy can cause economic depressions, and foster the avoidance of taxation, it remains unregulated because of the wealth and influence of those who comprise it.

In fiscal year 2020 we incurred a federal deficit of $3.1 trillion. We have incurred a cumulative deficit of almost $28 trillion. Further, Social Security, Medicare and Medicaid are all headed for insolvency when our children and grandchildren will need them. The needed reforms are not on our politicians' agendas, because the wealthy, exercising undue influence, don't need Social Security, Medicare and Medicaid. Further, reducing the national debt would encroach on their incomes and wealth. See Chapter 16, THE NATIONAL DEBT: STUDENT DEBT.

Rather than legislating against the undue influence and political corruption, many in Congress have become a part of it. Rather than focusing on the concentration of wealth, many in Congress have benefitted from it. The enactment of the 2017 Tax Cuts and Jobs Act benefitted corporations and the wealthy, while increasing the national debt for our children and grandchildren. Among many other benefits granted the wealthy, it reduced the corporate tax rate from 35 percent to 21 percent. While the tax cuts were palmed off on the gullible and powerless public as a means to stimulate the economy by hiring more workers, a December 2020 study by the London School of Economics showed that tax cuts consistently benefit the wealthy. The Washington Post reported on a Forbes study showing that as a result the number of billionaires increased by 660 persons in 2020 from 2,095 to 2,755, more than substantiating the London School of Economics' study.

The 2020 $1.4 trillion spending legislation approved by Congress benefitted the healthcare industry with $375 billion in tax cuts. Industry patent protection was increased from five to twelve years for "chemically synthesized polypeptide" drugs insuring higher drug prices for an additional seven years. Yet, congress failed the public by not limiting surprise medical bills from out of network providers. It also failed to limit prescription drug price increases to the inflation index. Large, wealthy hospital systems who suspended elective procedures are coming out of the pandemic better off financially than before. See Chapter 13, HEALTH CARE. While workers were given the choice of returning to life threatening work conditions, or losing their unemployment compensation, many corporations and big businesses were getting the hand-out socialism from the government they hate, while imposing the capitalism they extol on their workers.

The concentration of wealth resulting from undue influence in government policies can be illustrated very simply. Though there were many more two-person working households in 2018 when compared to 1989, the median household income for 2018 was only $63,517 compared to $57,059 in 1989, adjusted for inflation. Essentially, working folk were no better off in 2018, than working folk were 29 years ago; even with two persons working in each household.

For the same 29-year period the DOW Jones Industrial Average (DJIA) increased from 2,753 at the close of 1989 to 23,062 at the close of 2018; about an 837% increase. The value of publicly traded corporations grew 76 times faster than household median income. The increased wealth generally benefitted the top executives of large corporations and large shareholders; not their workers. The value of privately held corporations grew even faster than publicly held corporations. Further the DJIA doesn't reflect the wealth of the shadow economy, because few, if any, of these businesses are listed there. These issues are discussed in Chapter 10, UNDUE INFLUENCE: THE CONCENTRATION OF WEALTH.

Rather than controlling our military interventions and killings, Congress has shirked its exclusive constitutional power to declare war. Al Qaeda in Afghanistan was defeated. Osama Bin Laden was killed. Saddam Hussein in Iraq was deposed and killed. These wars have continued contrary to our nation's best interests, but very much in the interests of military contractors who received $370 billion in 2019. There were 50,000 contractor employees in the Middle East in 2019 versus 35,000 military personnel. Congress has not authorized the continued military actions and killings in Afghanistan or Iraq, or the U.S. military actions in Syria, Yemen, Libya, Somalia, among others. Congress has allowed troops with nebulous missions and unknown expenses to be stationed in 170 countries. These issues are discussed in Chapter 14, MILITARY INTERVENTION AND KILLINGS.

St. Thomas Aquinas provided the outlines of the Just War Theory. Under the Just War Theory, the reasons for going to war must be met, otherwise the killings are murders. In 1993 the U.S. Catholic Conference stated that, *"Force maybe used only to correct a grave public evil, for example, aggression or massive violation of the basic human rights of whole populations. Only duly constituted public authorities may wage war."*

Many of our military's killings are based on intelligence from individuals, groups, or tribes cooperating with the United States for a price, but feuding with other individuals, groups, or tribes that become targets. A purse snatcher can't be arrested without probable cause, nor imprisoned without a fair trial, but a person or group accused of being a threat to the United States on questionable grounds has no recourse before being killed suddenly in their own country, thousands of miles away, because of an unspecified grudge that becomes "intelligence."

More frequent and more severe hurricanes, tornados, floods, droughts, and a more than a doubling of the days in the Forest Service's fire seasons can be shown to result from global warming and climate change, which are exacerbated by fossil fuel combustion, poor methane leakage management policies and other human caused factors. Our national policies are greatly influenced by the businesses and corporations whose activities promote global warming and climate change. See Chapter 15, THE ENVIRONMENT: HEALTH AND LONGEVITY.

Businesses under the guise of protecting the public are only too happy to lobby for three-strikes for life-in-prison, limited parole, and privately managed prisons; neglecting the injustices and social cost of having two million persons incarcerated. See Chapter 17, PRISON REFORM.

Thirty thousand annual gun deaths are a significant national issue. See Chapter 19, GUN SAFETY. Is the Food Safety and Inspection Service (FSIS) looking out for our food safety, or the profits of the industries it's supposed to regulate? See Chapter 12, FOOD SAFETY.

As stated above, Jesus emphasized loving our neighbors as ourselves, living by the golden rule, being magnanimous to those who ask of us, caring about the poor, the afflicted, the imprisoned, by acting and giving, not just remuneration from our abundance, but giving time, effort and love, with self-sacrifice to those from whom no love, return or remuneration is sought, quietly and without notoriety. These requirements have not been adapted to today's world. They have been relegated to near obscurity and insignificance by many of today's churches, seminaries and by many of Jesus' alleged followers.

Who is doing the will of the Father in heaven in today's world? Who are today's Christian heretics?

Chapter 1

THE BIBLE: HISTORICAL CONTEXT: INERRANCY

If the Bible is the literal, inerrant word of God, as many Christians believe, then God intended humans to forever continually debate what he intended in the 66 books and 783 pages in the New Revised Standard Version of the Bible. There is no intent to denigrate the beauty, truths, or sacredness of what the biblical authors wrote. Nevertheless, at the time the New Testament was imposed in the late fourth century, the biblical authors had written their books, gospels and letters for multiple reasons, in diverse locations, decades apart; and in the case of the Old Testament, centuries apart. The New Testament writers had no idea that what they wrote would, some three centuries later, be compiled into a single document that was intended to express a singular view of God and Jesus. Not surprisingly, the single document has its share of inconsistencies and ambiguities. Further, the fundamental Christian concepts of the "Holy Trinity" and "original sin" are not mentioned in the Bible. These concepts and beliefs were not developed until centuries after Jesus and the biblical texts were written.

Today's Bibles do not contain the inerrant word of God, because original manuscripts no longer exist. See the subchapter below entitled, Bibles Before the Year 1,000. The original manuscripts have been copied, recopied and recopied an uncounted number of times by ancient scribes who introduced errors, their own interpretations, and their own revisions and corrections. Many biblical experts believe that the story of the adulterous woman was not included in the Gospel of John until the Middle-Ages. Most biblical scholars believe the longer ending in the Gospel of Mark (16:9-18) was not included in the oldest manuscripts available. Even in our own times, new biblical interpretations and versions are continually created and published. What is happening today is essentially a continuation of the process that began with the copying of the original manuscripts almost 2,000 years ago in an age before the Gutenberg printing press was invented in 1,450.

Prior to studying the Bible it is important to understand that there are writings in many ancient civilizations other than Judaism that relate to the creation and the beginnings, great floods, the human journey, life, death and the hereafter. The writings in the subchapter below entitled, Ancient Writings and the Bible, are a small sample of the writings from ancient civilizations other than Judaism. Many, predate the biblical narratives, and are only a fraction of those in existence, indicating that the biblical narratives are not necessarily original or unique.

It is also important to understand that Jesus' early followers held a wide diversity of beliefs about Jesus and his nature, as indicated in the subchapter below entitled, Beliefs of the Early Followers of Jesus. These beliefs were stamped out by Church of Rome authorities who had little tolerance for divergent views and beliefs, particularly since the church was continually in the process of developing its own beliefs. As indicated in the PREFACE, what emerged during the stamping out of these beliefs and the development of new beliefs is essentially today's Nicene form of Christianity.

Nicene Christianity emphasizes and promotes Jesus' deity, the Holy Trinity, the Nicene Creed, human sinfulness, and Jesus' death and resurrection. Paul's letters, Acts and the Gospel of John need to be understood in the context in which they were written, as discussed in Chapter 2, THE APOSTLE PAUL AND ACTS, Chapter 3, ORIGINAL SIN, and Chapter 4, THE HISTORICAL CONTEXT OF THE GOSPEL OF JOHN. Nicene Christianity largely ignores the reason for Jesus' very being and ministry as expressed in the synoptic gospels of Mark, Matthew and Luke that emphasize loving our neighbors as ourselves, living by the golden rule, being magnanimous to those who ask of us, caring about the poor, the afflicted, the imprisoned, by acting and giving, not just remuneration from our abundance, but giving time, effort and love, with self-sacrifice to those from whom no love, return or remuneration is sought, quietly and without notoriety.

Ancient Writings and the Bible

The Old Testament includes accounts of monotheism, creation, the Garden of Eden, great floods, the infant Moses' rescue from a bitumen sealed basket floating in the Nile River, and other events that are similar to those included in the literature of the Babylonians, Assyrians, Egyptians, Greeks and Chinese civilizations. Humankind apparently has many similar thought processes relating to matters such as the beginnings, the meaning of life, and the hereafter. When the literature of ancient civilizations is studied, these traits can readily be seen.

Monotheism was first recognized in Egypt during the reign of Akhenaten who worshiped, Aten, the sun god in the 14th century BCE. Worship of other gods was banned, though the ban proved unpopular with the Egyptian priestly classes. There is no archaeological evidence that monotheism was widespread in the ancient lands of Israel or Judah. There is archaeological evidence edited out of the Bible that suggests that as late as the 8th century BCE, Yahweh was married to the goddess

Asherah. The gods Ba'al, Marduk, Ashur and others were worshiped in ancient Israel and Judah.

Many ancient civilizations have a creation story. The Garden of Eden story has elements of an earlier written Sumerian text regarding the Dieties, Enki and Ninhursag. This account is about creation and a garden of paradise known as Dilmun created primarily by the feminine Diety Ninhursag. Enki engorges himself on plants he shouldn't have eaten, and is afflicted with enduring pain all over his body. In healing Enki's pain by taking away and experiencing the pain herself, Ninhursag gives birth to the entity, Ninti, "the Lady of the Rib", who gives life. It is interesting that the Garden of Eden story has Adam and Eve being afflicted for eating fruit they shouldn't have eaten, and Eve being created and given life from Adam's rib, of all the anatomy that could have been chosen for creating a new human being.

Ancient Chinese texts portrayed a mix of historical events and legends in the records of China's first dynasty, that of the Xia. These texts contain stories of a great flood with a Noah type of savior, the Emperor Yu, who gained the mandate of heaven after dredging canals to drain the floodwaters. Some dismissed the Emperor Yu story as a myth. However, recent archaeological evidence supports the flood portion of the story as a historical account. Chinese scientists recently found evidence of a catastrophic flood that overwhelmed the Yellow River valley in China 4,000 years ago. Unlike the Noah flood that was created by 40 days of rain, the Yellow River flood was caused by an earthquake that created a landslide that blocked the river. The river then crested over the blockage and drove the blockage downstream.

There are other great flood tales in antiquity predating the biblical account of the Noah flood, including the earliest known, which was Tablet XI of the Gilgamesh Epic about Utnapishtim. The Gilgamesh Epic was a part of the discovery of the Sumerian civilization dating back to 3,500 BCE in Mesopotamia. The Sumerians had the earliest known form of writing. The Sumerians were superseded by the Babylonian and Assyrian civilizations. Another great flood story is recorded in the records of Assyrian antiquity as reported in George Smith's Assyrian Discoveries, in part as follows:

A ship thou shalt make

Into the deep launch it

Into the midst of it thy grain and goods

The animals all I will gather

And they shall be enclosed in thy door

All I possessed I caused to go into the ship

I entered into the midst of the ship and shut my door

The raging of the storm in the morning arose

The bright earth to a waste was turned

The deluge over the people reached to heaven

The seventh day the storm was calmed

I opened the window, light broke over my face

On the seventh day I sent forth a dove

I sent forth the animals to the four winds

I built an alter on the peak of the mountain

Biblical scholar, Professor Bart Ehrman, writes that Greek literature includes the story of a mother-to-be who was visited by a spirit from heaven who told her she would give birth to a son of a god. His birth was attended by supernatural signs. He became a child prodigy, impressing the religious leaders of his day. He traveled and engaged in an itinerant preaching ministry, urging people to give up their quest for power and material things, and concern themselves with their spiritual life.

He performed miracles; healing the sick, casting out demons, and raising the dead. He acquired many followers who were convinced he was divine. His enemies brought charges against him before the Roman authorities. After he died some of his followers claimed they saw him alive after he ascended into heaven. His followers wrote books about him. His name was Apollonius of Tyana, a philosopher and a worshiper of Greek gods, who lived about the time of Jesus. His followers knew about Jesus, but considered him to be a magician.

Most of what is known of Apollonius of Tyana comes from Greek sophist, Philostratus, who wrote an eight-volume biography of Apollonius about 220 CE at the request of empress Domna. Apollonius lived sometime between 3 BCE and 97 CE. He was born about the same time as Jesus, but of a wealthy family. Apollonius was active in Greece and Turkey, but traveled to Spain, Africa, Mesopotamia, India and allegedly confronted Emperor Nero in Rome.

Apollonius was credited with the performance of miracles and having extra-sensory perception in that he was able to predict events before they occurred. He was credited with many writings and letters, with some lost, and others preserved as fragments of disputed authenticity. Many comparisons have been between Jesus and Apollonius. One stark contrast is that Jesus' encounter with Roman authorities ended with Jesus' crucifixion, whereas Apollonius' encounter with emperors Nero and Domitian, left Apollonius unscathed. Such stories were not unusual 2,000 years ago in the polytheistic world of the ancients, since the boundary between mortal and immortal beings or divine beings was bridgeable, unlike the chasm that exists for modern Christians, a chasm bridged only by one's death.

Many historical and biblical scholars note the similarity of the Old Testament narration of the birth of Moses with an earlier Mesopotamian text about the birth of Sargon of Akkad, and the first great empire in history. Sargon lived about 1,000 years before Moses. He first conquered all of Mesopotamia, extending his empire to Persia in the east, and to the Mediterranean Sea and Asia Minor in the west. Sargon's many achievements resulted in considerable legend, which have been preserved not only in the language of the Acadians, but also in the languages of the Hittites. The story of Sargon is as follows:

Sargon the powerful king, the king of Akkadia am I

my mother was poor and born out of wedlock, my father I knew not;

the brother of my father lived in the mountains...

My mother, who was poor, secretly gave birth to me;

because of the oppressive king, she placed me in a basket of reeds,

she shut up the mouth of it in bitumen,

she abandoned me to the river, which did not overwhelm me.

The river bore me away and brought me to Akki the irrigator.

Akki the irrigator received me in the goodness of his heart.

Akki the irrigator reared me to boyhood.

Akki the irrigator made me a gardener.

My service as a gardener was pleasing to Ishtar and I became king.

—Wells, H. G., (1920). *The Outline of History*, Volume I,

p. 206.

In Exodus 2, Moses is abandoned by his biological mother because the Pharaoh decreed that the first-born Hebrew children should be killed because the Hebrews were becoming too numerous in Egypt. Moses' mother placed him in a reed basket, sealed it with bitumen, and floated him down the Nile where he was found and adopted by Pharaoh's daughter. Moses is then raised to maturity and allegedly leads the Israelites out of Egyptian slavery to the promised-land. Sargon was rescued from the Euphrates, Moses from the Nile. Sargon came under the protection of the Babylonian Goddess of love and fertility, Ishtar, and Moses came under the protection of Pharaoh's daughter. Both baskets were sealed with bitumen.

As indicated above, these are only a few examples of ancient literature pre-dating and containing narratives similar to biblical accounts indicating that the biblical narratives may not be original or unique.

Beliefs of the Early Followers of Jesus

This subchapter describes the beliefs of a few of the many groups of the early followers of Jesus. Jesus' early followers held a wide diversity of beliefs about Jesus, the nature of Jesus, and Jesus' ministry. Before Christianity became the official religion of the Roman Empire, like Rome itself, the Roman church's hierarch acquired the influence and power to stamp out what it considered errant beliefs as heretical, even as the church itself was developing its own beliefs. Heresy at that time meant excommunication and relegation of the souls of the excommunicated individuals to hell. Today's Christianity allows salvation and achieving the kingdom of heaven somewhat independent of official church doctrine, though some churches may not agree.

This subchapter deals with the diversity of beliefs primarily during the first four centuries CE. Though the Arian controversy dealing with the divinity of Jesus occurred during this time frame, the Arian controversy is best dealt with separately in Chapter 4, "THE HISTORICAL CONTEXT OF THE GOSPEL of JOHN." Also, although the genesis of the controversy over justification by faith, and justification by faith alone that lead to the Protestant Reformation also arose during the first four centuries, it is best dealt with separately in Chapter 5, "THE REFORMATION: JUSTIFICATION BY FAITH ALONE: PREDESTINATION"

The Ebionites and The Letter of James

It is overly simplistic and easy to simply dismiss the views of the early followers of Jesus from the perspective of present-day Christianity. These followers were persons who might have known Jesus, or known persons who had known Jesus. Jewish followers of Jesus would have a different perspective than Gentile followers. Heritage and nationality would have an impact, as well as literacy or the lack of it. Jesus' death and resurrection are believed to have occurred about 30 CE. Paul's first letter was written about 50 CE. In the meantime and during Paul's ministry, the Jerusalem church was active, and led by Jesus' brother James.

The Ebionites were Jewish followers of Jesus who might have originally been a part of the Jerusalem church, but eventually separated from it. The Ebionites accepted poverty, and believed that Jesus was the Messiah. They rejected any thoughts of Jesus' divinity, since Jesus was the son of Joseph and Mary within the Davidic lineage. Any follower of Jesus must fulfill the laws of Moses. The members of the Jerusalem church were believed to be the direct disciples of Jesus, and led by Jesus' brother, James. Peter and John were also probably members of the Jerusalem church, though perhaps not Ebionites. The Letters of Paul and the Book of Acts mentions the Jerusalem church (Acts 8:1-3, 1 Corinthian 16:1-4, Romans 15:14-32).

Though there was considerable opposition, jailings and beatings of Jesus' disciples in and around Jerusalem by Jews who were not followers of Jesus, Peter and John's efforts brought some success in converting Jews, Acts 4:1-3, 10-12, 5:14-16, 41. The Letter of James is explicitly contrary to Paul's expressed beliefs and teaching that faith in Jesus as Lord and Savior alone was enough to ensure salvation. The Letter of James is also contrary to the later teachings that underpinned the Reformation that faith alone is sufficient for salvation. James states:

> be doers of the word, not merely hearers who deceive themselves. For if any are hearers and not doers, they are like those who look in the mirror, for they look at themselves and, on going away, immediately forget what they were like. But those who look into the perfect law, the law of liberty, and persevere, being not hearers who forget, but doers who act—they will be blessed in their doing...

You shall love your neighbor as yourself ...

What good is it, my brothers and sisters if you say you have faith, but do not have works? Can faith save you? If a brother or sister is naked and lacks daily food, and one of you says to them, go in peace; keep warm and eat your fill, and yet you do not supply their bodily needs, what is the good of that? So faith by itself if it has no works is dead ...

Show me your faith apart from works, and I by my works will show you my faith ...

Was not our ancestor Abraham justified by works when he offered his son, Isaac on the alter? You see that faith was active along with his works. Thus the scripture was fulfilled that says, "Abraham believed God, and it was reckoned to him as righteousness," and he was called a friend of God. You see that a person is justified by works and not be faith alone, James 1–2:24.

The beginning of the demise of the Jerusalem church might be what was described in Acts 8:1. Saul approved the killing of the martyr Stephen. A severe persecution was perpetrated against the Jerusalem church, and all but the apostles became scattered through the countryside. Saul went from house to house dragging off the men and women and committing them to jail. Two decades later in 70 CE, as a part of putting down the Jewish revolt, the Romans invaded Jerusalem and destroyed the temple accelerating the transformation of Judaism from a sacrificial religion to a Torah study religion. The Roman invasion of Jerusalem and the destruction of the temple no doubt had a negative effect on the Jerusalem church whose members may have been forced to scatter.

The Ebionites are mentioned by the early church bishops who considered their practices and beliefs to be errant and heretical. It would appear that Jesus and his nature would be better known by his brother, James, and other close followers than more distant persons. However, because the Ebionites were under stress from Jews who considered their beliefs that Jesus was the Messiah to be blasphemous, and because of the pressure by the early church bishops who were Gentiles and bent on creating a deity of Jesus, the Jerusalem church, and the Ebionites who probably were a part of the Jerusalem church, eventually ceased to exist. However, scattered but unsubstantiated accounts of their continued presence exist centuries later.

The Marcionites

The second century Marcionites believed that the death and resurrection of Jesus represented a different god than the allegedly inferior, Old Testament god. They believed that Jesus' disciples never understood Jesus' nature even after his death and resurrection. Imagine that? Marcionites believed that Jesus' disciples continued to be followers of the Old Testament, Jewish god, perhaps having in mind the Jerusalem church. The Marcionites comprised a large following of Jesus. They compiled their own Bible comprised of abbreviated versions of Luke and Paul's letters.

They considered the Old Testament God to be merciless, when compared to Jesus. Who could blame them? For example, at the behest of the Old Testament god, all the inhabitants of the Canaanite town Of Ai, men and women were slaughtered, their livestock taken, and the town burned, Joshua 8:24-30. The ancient Israelites occupied the land on which they had not labored, towns they had not built, and ate and harvested food they had not worked for, Joshua 24:13. Further, the Old Testament God in Leviticus 21:16-23 prohibited anyone who was blind, lame, or had a deformity, a hunchback, a dwarf, blemished eyes, an itching disease, scabs or crushed testicles from coming near the curtain of the temple, approaching the alter, or otherwise profaning the Lord's sanctuaries. Perhaps, the Marcionites can be excused for considering the Old Testament god as a merciless, different god from the god represented by Jesus.

The Marcionites believed in a New Testament Jesus representing a more benevolent god who heals the infirm, the leper, the blind, and the lame. The Marcionites believed that Jesus had to return to Earth as a vision to reveal the truth to Paul. This is why, as the Marcionites explained, Paul had to confront Peter's and James' views, as in Galatians 2:1-15 and Acts 15:1-21, that it was not necessary to obey the Law, that Peter and James were apostles to the circumcised, while Paul was the apostle for the uncircumcised.

Eventually, the Marcionites lost favor with the church in Rome, and with followers believing that the Old and New Testament God is the same God. The single deity believers disparaged Marcionite dogma, and exerted pressure against followers of Marcionite beliefs and writings. The church in Rome concluded that the older history attributed to what we now call the Old Testament was a more palatable alternative to the Pagan religions of the Romans, Greeks and Egyptians than the two-god Marcionite beliefs. Moreover, Jesus and Paul were inextricably tied to ancient Judaism. Thus, it became increasingly difficult to simply dismiss the Old Testament god as a different god. Though originally large in numbers, as a consequence of the pressure of the church in Rome which was becoming ever more powerful and the center for Christianity, the Marcionite beliefs eventually ceased to exist.

Manichaeism

St. Augustine, the influential fourth century Christian theologian, helped develop the concepts of the Holy Trinity and Original Sin, among other Christian dogma. It is interesting to note that St. Augustine was at one time in his life a believer in Manichaeism, a religion allegedly based on Jesus' statements in the gospel of John, where Jesus says:

I will ask the Father, and he will give you another Advocate, to be with you forever. This is the Spirit of truth, whom the world cannot receive, because it neither sees him nor knows him, because he abides with you, and he will be in you. John 14:16-17....In a little while the world will no longer see me, but you will see me: because I live, you also will live. John 14:19. But the Advocate, the Holy Spirit (or Helper), whom the Father will send in my name will teach you everything. John 14:26...it is to your advantage that I go away, for if I do not go away, the Advocate will not come to you....I still have many things to say to you, but you cannot hear them now. When the Spirit of truth comes, he will guide you into all the truth...(John 16:7, 12-13).

The believers of Manichaeism were not necessarily followers of Jesus. Mani, born about 216 CE, was instilled in the Judeo-Christian faiths and considered himself to be an Advocate. Mani considered the teachings of Buddha, Zoroaster and Jesus to have been incomplete. Manichaeans believed Jesus was wholly divine, never experiencing conception or human birth. Since he was a light to the world, where was the light while he was in the womb? Jesus the Messiah was truly born at his baptism when the Father acknowledged Jesus as his son. The suffering, death and resurrection of Jesus were appearances only, exemplary of the suffering and eventual deliverance of the human soul.

Mani preached Manichaeism as a dualistic cosmology that described the struggle between a good, spiritual world of light, and a dark materialistic world of darkness. In this respect Manichaeism was similar to the beliefs of Christian Gnostics (see below) who represented a large following of Jesus during this period. Manichaeism thrived between the third and 14th century. It existed from as far east as China until about the 14th century, and as far west as portions of the Roman Empire. Manichaeism was a rival to Christianity for supplanting the ancient pagan religions.

The Gospel of Peter

The Gospel of Peter was widely accepted and relied upon by many followers of Jesus. Peter included an account of Jesus' resurrection and the emergence of Jesus from the tomb. The Gospel of Peter was referred to in early Christian written accounts and was in wide use in Christian churches into the second century. It includes an account that the cross was questioned and spoke.

Significantly, the Gospel of Peter includes a description of Jesus' crucifixion, and the fact that Jesus did not appear to be enduring pain. This passage supported the interpretation by many followers that Jesus had a divine nature, as opposed to a human nature, and that therefore, he would not have suffered. This concept by many followers was that Jesus' body and worldly appearance and actions were simply an appearance by a divine being. These beliefs were very similar to the beliefs of many of the Gnostic followers of Jesus discussed below.

Other followers of Jesus thought that Jesus was both human and divine, but not at the same time; perhaps relying on the Gospel of Mark. As stated below, in Mark the spirit descended on Jesus like a dove, Mark 1:10-11, but left Jesus on the cross, Mark 15:34. These followers of Jesus were labeled as Docetists by the early church fathers and were prosecuted for their allegedly errant beliefs. The Gospel of Peter was most probably rejected for inclusion into the New Testament, because it did not fit the prevailing view at that time that although Jesus was of a divine nature, he suffered during the crucifixion.

The Christian Gnostics

One very large and influential group was the Christian Gnostics, who held a diversity of beliefs. The Christian Gnostics were among the better educated and literate followers of Jesus. They were unwilling to accept the narrowly defined church beliefs emanating from the church in Rome, which had the Roman Empire imprimatur behind them, both before and after the Romans themselves officially adopted Christianity.

Indeed, as an indication of the intention of the church in Rome to assert its authority over other churches, as early as the late first century or early second century, Clement, apparently an official in the church in Rome, sent a letter to the church in Corinth strongly urging the church to restore deposed leaders of the Corinthian church to their former positions. The rationale in the letter was that the original appointees were apostles, none of whom had been charged with moral offenses. It is not known if the Corinthian church complied with the letter.

Irenaeus of Lyon was the primary Gnostic Christian prosecutor. Until 1945 Irenaeus' "Against Heresies," was the best surviving description of Gnosticism. The establishment church had stamped out Gnostic Christian believers and destroyed Gnostic writing. However, in 1945 in the Nag Hammadi region of upper Egypt, two brothers, peasants, digging for nitrates to fertilize their crops, came across what was described as a large sealed jar containing books and papyrus fragments. The writings were probably hidden and preserved by Christian Gnostics after the church hierarchy ordered the suppression of Gnostic writings and beliefs.

Based on the Nag Hammadi findings, many biblical scholars have concluded that much of what Irenaeus wrote about Gnosticism was inaccurate to show Gnosticism in an unfavorable light. One example is that Irenaeus described Gnostics as sexual libertines when many Gnostic writings advocated chastity. However, Gnostic Christians were not a single group with monolithic beliefs. The general editor of the Nag Hammadi Library, James M. Robinson, points to Timothy 2:16-18 as indicative of the tensions between Gnosticism and the church hierarchy, where Hymenaeus and Philetus are disparaged for preaching that the resurrection of believers had taken place.

Christian Gnostics' contrary views of the Church in Rome is demonstrated in "The Apocalypse of Peter," where Peter is witnessing dual images of a Jesus being nailed to the cross and a Jesus above the cross. Jesus above the cross alludes to the fact that only his physical likeness is put to death and that his spirit is beyond pain and death. Christian Gnostics believed that salvation comes by the spirit (soul) escaping the body and reuniting with the Pleroma, essentially, God's heavenly universe, sharing this very wide spread belief with followers of Manichaeism

In the Second Treatise of the Great Seth, Jesus speaks to his followers describing his empowerment as an undefiled spirit sent to reveal the truth. Jesus refutes the church at the time that is claiming to be advancing Jesus' interests. Similar to the Apocalypse of Peter, Jesus died only in appearance. It was Simon who bore the cross on his shoulders and Jesus was transformed with Simon of Cyrene. In Mark 15:21, Simon is compelled to carry Jesus' cross. The Second Treatise of the Great Seth corroborates the lost writings of Basilides who also wrote that Jesus changed identities with Simon of Cyrene. Thus, Simon of Cyrene was crucified, not Jesus. Despite the persecutions by the church at the time, purportedly advancing the causes of Jesus, many Gnostics believed that only Gnostic believers would enjoy eternal life.

As stated in The Gnostic Society Library, An Introduction to Gnosticism and The Nag Hammadi Library, see http://www.gnosis. org/naghamm/intro.html:

> In the first century of the Christian era, this term, Gnostic, began to be used to denote a prominent segment of…the diverse new Christian community. Among these earlier followers of Christ, it appears that an elite group delineated themselves…by claiming not simply a belief in Christ and his message, but a "special witness" or revelatory experience of the divine. It was this experience, this gnosis, which… set the true follower apart from his fellows.

In the initial decades of the Christian church...no orthodoxy, or single acceptable format of Christian thought had yet been defined... That Gnosticism was, at least briefly, in the mainstream of Christianity is witnessed by the fact that one of the most prominent...Gnostic teachers, Valentinus, may have been in consideration during the mid-second century for election to the Bishop of Rome....A prime characteristic of the Gnostics was their propensity for claiming to be keepers of secret teachings and gospels....Though an influential member of the Roman church in the mid-second century, by the end of his life some 20 years later [Valentinus] had been forced from the public eye and branded a heretic...

Gnosticism's secret knowledge, its continuing revelations and production of new scripture, its aestheticism and paradoxically contrasting libertine postures, were met with increasing suspicion. By A.D. 180, Irenaeus, Bishop of Lyon, was publishing attacks on Gnosticism as heresy, a work that continued with increasing vehemence by the church in Rome.

The church in Rome was deeply and profoundly influenced by the struggle against Gnosticism in the second and third centuries. Formulations and many traditions in orthodox theology came as a reflection and shadows of the confrontation with the Gnosis.

But by the end of the fourth century the struggle with the classical Gnosticism represented in the Nag Hammadi texts was essentially over; the evolving orthodox ecclesia had added the force of political correctness to dogmatic denunciation, and with this sword so-called heresy was painfully cut from the Christian body. Gnosticism was eradicated, its remaining teachers murdered or driven into exile, and its sacred books destroyed. All that remained for scholars seeking to understand Gnosticism in later centuries were the denunciations and fragments preserved in the patristic heresiologies—or so it seemed, until a day in 1945.

The Three Synoptic Gospels of Mark, Matthew, Luke, and the Gospel of John

As stated above, even before Christianity became the official religion of the Roman Empire, like Rome itself, the church in Rome acquired the influence and power to promote its own views and to stamp out the wide diversity of beliefs of many of the early Christians. The church considered these allegedly errant beliefs as heretical. Heresy at that time meant excommunication and relegation of the souls of the excommunicated individuals to hell. Those accused of heresy sometimes leveled heresy allegations against their accusers.

There are 27 books comprising what we now call the New Testament. There are the four Gospels of Mark, Matthew, Luke and John, the Acts of the Apostles, 13 letters of the Apostle Paul, the letter to the Hebrews, the Letter of James, the two letters of Peter, the three letters of John, the letter of Jude and the Revelation of John. This subchapter is primarily, but briefly focused on the four gospels of Mark, Matthew, Luke and John.

According to biblical scholar Bart Ehrman, the evidence that the New Testament was to be limited, or imposed, was first indicated by a letter from Bishop Athanasius of Alexandria, Egypt, in 367 CE to his churches listing the 27 writings in their then existing form and directing that only these be used. Yes, this Athanasius is the same Athanasius that opposed Arius' views about Jesus in the PREFACE. According to Wikipedia the 27-book New Testament was formally canonized during the councils of Hippo, 393 CE, and Carthage, North Africa in 397 CE.

Regarding chronology, it is believed that Jesus was born about 4

BCE and died about 30 CE, some 1,990 years ago. The letters of the Apostle Paul are the oldest writings included in the New Testament. They are thought to have been written between 50-64 CE, about two to three decades after Jesus' crucifixion and resurrection, and shortly before the Gospel of Mark was written, about 65 CE.

Though 27 books and letters were included in the New Testament, the New Testament is also notable for the writings that were excluded. Bart Ehrman, in *Lost Christianities*, lists more than 40 books and letters that relate to early Christianity that were excluded from the New Testament. These include: Epistle of the Apostles, Gospel according to the Hebrews, Gospel of the Ebionites, Gospel of the Egyptians, Gospel of Mary, Gospel of the Nazarenes, Gospel of Nicodemus, Gospel of Peter, Gospel of Philip, Gospel of the Savior, Coptic Gospel of Thomas, Infancy Gospel of Thomas, Gospel of Truth, Papyrus Egerton, Proto Gospel of James, Secret Gospel of Mark, Acts of John, Acts of Paul, Acts of Peter, Acts of Pilate, Acts of Thecla, Acts of Thomas, 1 Clement, 2 Clement, 3 Corinthians, Correspondence of Paul and Seneca, The Didache, Epistle of Barnabas, Letter to the Laodiceans, Letter of Peter to James and its Reception, Letter of Ptolemy to Flora, The Preaching of Peter, Pseudo-Clementine Literature, Pseudo-Titus, Treatise on the Resurrection, Apocalypse of Paul, Apocalypse of Peter, Coptic Apocalypse of Peter, First Thought in Three Forms, Hymn of the Pearl, Origin of the World, Second Treatise of the Great Seth, Secret Book of John and Shepherd of Hermas.

Unlike the letters of the Apostle Paul who was literate, the Three Synoptic Gospels of Mark, Matthew and Luke, and the Gospel of John were all written anonymously in the third person. There is no persuasive evidence who actually wrote them. Acts 4:13 specifically describes Peter and John as illiterate. Given the occupations of Jesus' other disciples in that era, they were also likely to have been illiterate. They are the end products of what was probably a long oral and written tradition. Mark was the first gospel written about 65 CE. Matthew and Luke, acting independently, were written about 85 CE using Mark as a source and the "Q document" theorized to have existed and available at the time. The Q document is now lost. John was written about 95 CE. The naming ascribed to the gospels occurred after they were written during the second century

The language spoken by Jesus and the 12 disciples was Aramaic; not Hebrew, Greek or Latin. Aramaic came to be spoken in the Middle East sometime after the Persians defeated the Babylonians about 538 BCE. Yet, Greek formed the initial versions of the gospels and most of the writings in the New Testament. Original manuscripts no longer existed when the printing press was invented in the 15th century. What existed were hundreds of hand-written copies that had been recopied uncounted times by scribes who introduced their own errors and beliefs. These were what were mass produced.

In addition to the changes made to the gospel scripts after they were written, the accuracy and authenticity of the original gospel writers should not be overestimated. For example, the Gospel of Mark was written about 65 CE 30-years after the events described. This would have been similar to describing the Gulf of Tonkin incident, or the assassination of President Kennedy in the year 2000, by a person who might not have been born, did not witness the events, and had not read about them. There were no radios, libraries, internet search engines, TVs, newspapers, magazines, or even printing presses. The difficulties for the authors of Matthew, Luke and John would have been greater, because additional decades had elapsed.

Chapter 2, THE APOSTLE PAUL AND ACTS, deals with Paul's 13 letters, Paul's ministry, the inconsistencies between Paul's letters and Acts, and Acts' attempts to meld together Paul's ministry with Jesus' teachings and ministry. Chapter 3, ORIGINAL SIN, deals with the issue of original sin. Chapter 4, THE HISTORICAL CONTEXT

OF THE GOSPEL OF JOHN, provides the proper context for limiting the broad and pervasive influence John has been given in present day Christianity. Jesus' teachings and his ministry in conveying God's word are treated in Chapter 6, WHAT WERE JESUS' TEACHINGS and Chapter 7, THE LORD'S PRAYER. The description of the gospels here is limited to a few vignettes plus the gospels' respective descriptions of Jesus' origins, his trial, his crucifixion, resurrection and appearances.

The Gospel of Mark, the first gospel written to survive and perhaps the most accurate, was written about 65 CE, before the destruction of the second Jewish temple in Jerusalem in 70 CE. Mark does not mention the birth of Jesus. Mark begins with the baptism of Jesus by John the Baptist purporting to cleanse Jesus of his sins and causing the Spirit to descend on Jesus (Mark 1:9–11). Jesus is generally portrayed as without sin, thus the baptism by John is of questionable significance in that regard. Later, Peter, James and John witness Jesus' transfiguration. Jesus orders them to tell no one until after he is raised from the dead (Mark 9:2-8). Many early followers of Jesus interpreted the transfiguration as the beginning of the divinity portion of Jesus' life, which ended when the divinity left Jesus on the cross when he cried out, *"My God, my God, why have you forsaken me?"* (Mark 15:34).

Jesus is betrayed to the Jewish high priests by Judas, one of Jesus' twelve disciples. Jesus is then arrested and handed over to the high priests who accuse Jesus of blaspheme when he responds to their questions as to whether he is the blessed one. The priests handed Jesus over to Pontius Pilate, the Roman governor Of Judea at the time. When questioned by Pilate, Jesus provides no defense of himself. Though Pilate could see no wrong doing by Jesus, the priests stirred up the crowd to crucify Jesus, and though Pilate was reluctant to do so, he complied with demands of the high priests and the crowd. Jesus was crucified and died (Mark 14:43-15:39).

Many scholars believe the oldest manuscripts of Mark ended when Mary Magdalene, Mary, mother of James and Salome visit the tomb and found the stone rolled away. They were informed by a young man dressed in a white robe that Jesus had been raised, and that they should tell Jesus' disciples and Peter to go to Galilee where they will see Jesus. The women fled from the tomb in terror and amazement. They informed no one, because they were afraid (Mark 16:1-8). The longer ending of Mark in Mark 16:9-20, where Jesus appears to Mary Magdalene and later to the 11 disciples, is generally thought to have been added later by scribes.

Mark details the miracles performed by Jesus and the many parables and teachings he gave to his disciples. Jesus demanded secrecy from the disciples about the miracles they witnessed. The secrecy Jesus insisted upon regarding the miracles he performed in Mark are to be contrasted with the portrayal of Jesus in the gospel of John, below, written about 30 years after Mark, with Jesus claiming the miracles for all to see. Further, Mark has Jesus eating the Passover meal the evening before Passover, and Jesus' crucifixion as occurring the day of Passover (Mark 14:12–15:39). John describes Jesus' crucifixion as occurring the day before Passover, when the lambs were slaughtered in preparation for the Passover meal (John 19:14, 31).

The Gospel of Matthew is believed to have been written about 85 CE, after the destruction of the temple in Jerusalem by the Romans. Matthew cites many examples that Jesus is the Messiah called for by the Torah. For example, the Old Testament provides that the Messiah will be a descendant of David (Isaiah 11:1-2), and Matthew states that Jesus' birth fulfilled this prophesy. Matthew begins with the genealogy allegedly leading from King David to Jesus (Matthew 1:1-17). The Matthew genealogy is not consistent with the genealogies in 1 Chronicles 3:1-24, or Luke 3:23-38. In any event, according to the Matthew and Luke accounts of Jesus' birth, Jesus was conceived as a result of the union of Mary and the Holy Spirit, not by Joseph, or anyone in David's lineage (Matthew 1:18, Luke 1:34-35). Matthew portrays the birth of Jesus as related to the visit by the three wise men following the star to the location of Jesus' birth.

Another example of Matthew relating Jesus' birth to the Old Testament prophesies is the story of Joseph being instructed by an angel of the Lord to flee to Egypt with Jesus and Mary to avoid King Herod's order that all children two and under be killed. According to Matthew this was done to fulfill the Old Testament prophesy that *"Out of Egypt I have called my son"* (Matthew 2:13-15). Matthew is referring to Hosea 11:1-3, which states:

> When Israel was a child, I loved him, and out of Egypt I called my son. The more I called them, the more they went from me; they kept sacrificing to the Baals, and offering incense to idols. Yet it was I who taught Ephraim to walk, I took them up in my arms...

However, *"Ephraim"* was used by the Old Testament prophets as a symbol for the nation of Israel (Isaiah 7:2). When taken in its proper context, Hosea 11:1 is a lament by God about Israel's wayward ways at the time, which God likened to Ephraim. The reference to Ephraim in Hosea 11:1-3 is to Israel as God's son, and the exodus of Jews from Egypt, not to Jesus as God's son.

Matthew directly conflicts with the preaching and ministry of the Apostle Paul. Matthew states:

> Do not think that I have come to abolish the law or the prophets; I have come not to abolish but to fulfill. For truly I tell you, until heaven and earth pass away, not one letter, not on stroke of a letter, will pass from the law until all is accomplished. Therefore, whoever breaks one of the least of these commandments, and teaches others to do the same, will be called least in the king-

dom of heaven; but whoever does them and teaches them will be called great in the kingdom of heaven. For I tell you, unless your righteousness exceeds the scribes and Pharisees, you will never enter the kingdom of heaven (Matthew 5:17-20).

Paul preached that Jesus' death and resurrection supplanted the need to comply with the Law (Galatians 3:13-14, 23-27, 5:2-6; Romans 7:4-6).

Matthews' portrayal of Jesus betrayal by Judas, his trial before the high priests, and being handed over to Pontius Pilate is similar to Mark's. Again, Pilate was reluctant to punish Jesus, but did so because of the pressure from the priests, elders and the crowd that had been stirred up. Jesus was crucified and died (Matthew 26:47-27:54).

Matthew has Mary Magdalene and the "other Mary" visiting the tomb, when suddenly there was a great earth quake with an angel descending from heaven who rolled away the stone. His appearance was lightening and his clothing was white. He told them not to be afraid and advised that Jesus had been raised from the dead. He told them to tell the disciples, and that Jesus was going ahead of them to Galilee. The women left the tomb with fear and great joy and ran to tell the disciples, when Jesus appeared to them. Guards who had been guarding the tomb told the chief priests what had happened. The priests and elders gave the guards money and advised them to say that Jesus' disciples had stolen the body. The eleven disciples saw Jesus in Galilee, where Jesus baptized them and directing them to make disciples of all nations (Matthew 28:1-20).

The Gospel of Luke was written about 85 CE. Specifically, Luke states:

Since many have undertaken to set down an orderly account of the events that have been fulfilled among us, just as they were handed on to us by those who from the beginning were eyewitnesses and servants of the word, I too decided…to write an orderly account for you, most excellent Theophilus (Luke 1:1-3).

Theophilus is an unknown person in history and in the Bible. The writer of Luke also wrote Acts of the Apostles. The writer of Acts, presumed to be the same writer as the writer of Luke, also mentions Theophilus as below:

In the first book, Theophilus, I wrote about all that Jesus did and taught from the beginning until the day when he was taken up to heaven… (Acts 1:1-2).

Luke's portrayal of Jesus' birth as attended by shepherds, with Jesus being taken to Jerusalem by Joseph and Mary for circumcision (Luke 2:8-22), is not reconcilable with the Matthew version of Jesus' birth attended by three wise men, with Jesus being taken to Egypt until the death of Herod. Luke also details the birth of John the Baptist and the relationship between John the Baptist and Jesus. Luke's genealogy conflicts with Matthew's.

Luke's portrayal of Jesus' betrayal by Judas, his trial before the high priests, and being handed over to Pontius Pilate are similar to Mark's. Again, Pilate was reluctant to punish Jesus, but did so because of the pressure from the priests, elders and the crowd that had been stirred up. Jesus was crucified and died. One difference in Luke's portrayal of Jesus' trial from the Mark and Matthew portrayals is the involvement of Herod, the Jewish ruler of Palestine. After questioning Jesus before his accusers, Pilate sent Jesus and his accusers to Herod, apparently hoping to have Herod adjudicate Jesus' guilt. Herod after questioning Jesus before his accusers returned Jesus to Pilate (Luke 22:47-23:47).

Luke describes the women as visiting the tomb and finding the stone rolled away, but does not name them. Suddenly, two men with dazzling clothes stood beside them terrifying the women. The men reminded the women of Jesus' words stating "the Son of Man must be handed over to sinners, and be crucified and on the third day rise." It was Mary Magdalene, Joanna, Mary the mother of James and the other women with them who told the disciples. The disciples did not believe, but Peter ran to the tomb. He saw the linen cloths and went home amazed. In Luke's portrayal Jesus first appears to Cleopas and another (perhaps Simon, though unclear) on their way to Emmaus about seven miles from Jerusalem. Though they did not recognize Jesus at first, they eventually did. The two found the eleven and their companions and related that they had seen the risen Jesus. Jesus then stood among them. They were startled and terrified and thought they were seeing a ghost. Jesus showed them his wounds and opened their minds to the meaning of the scriptures. Jesus led them to Bethany, and after blessing them, was carried up into heaven (Luke 24:1-24:52).

The Gospel of John was written about 95 CE. Like the other gospels, the writer or writers of John are unknown. The Gospel of John is very much an original work. Though beautifully written, it does not rely on the three synoptic gospels that preceded it. In many respects John contradicts and reinterprets the earlier, and probably more reliable synoptic gospels that corroborate each other in relating the nature of Jesus. There are strong anti-Semitic sentiments in John suggesting that John was written as a reaction to the more formalized schism that arose between Jews, on the one hand, and Gentile and Jewish followers of Jesus, in the late first century when John was written. Chapter 4, THE HISTORICAL CONTEXT OF THE GOSPEL OF JOHN discusses these issues.

The author of John does not relate the events as in the synoptic gospels. A decade or more later than Matthew and Luke, and three decades later than the Gospel of Mark, John reinterprets and contradicts the events. Jesus' concern with secrecy in Mark must be contrasted with John, where the author immediately proclaims the identity of Jesus as

God, contrary to the three synoptic gospels. The miracles performed by Jesus, rather than being hidden or accomplished in secret, as related by Jesus' disciples, are performed in the open before audiences to prove the divinity of Jesus to all those present.

Regarding Jesus, John proclaims that "In the beginning was the Word and the Word was with God... And the Word became flesh and lived among us, and we have seen his glory (John 1:1-1:14). John, like the other gospels has Judas betraying Jesus, but unlike the synoptic gospels where Jesus displays fear of his future, but obedience to God, in John Jesus is eager to fulfill his destiny. Thus here, Judas is simply playing an essential part in Jesus' crucifixion. In John, Peter denies Jesus three times, but under different circumstances than in the synoptic gospels. Jesus is convicted before the high priest who brings Jesus to Pilate. Pilate states that the Jews should try Jesus under their own laws, but the priests claim that only the Romans have the authority to put anyone to death. John, unlike the other gospels has Pilate flogging Jesus before offering Him back to the Jews. The chief priests and the crowd shouted that Jesus should be crucified. Jesus was crucified and died. In John Jesus never cried out asking why God had forsaken him. In John, Jesus simply bows his head and gives up his spirit (John 13:21-19:30).

John has Joseph of Arimathea and Nicodemus claiming Jesus' body from Pilate and burying Jesus. Mary Magdalene was the first to visit the tomb and found the stone rolled away. She went running to Simon Peter, who went to the tomb with the other disciples. They found the linen wrappings, but not Jesus. Mary, when weeping outside the tomb, saw two angels dressed in white. After turning around she saw Jesus, thinking he was the gardener at first. After recognizing Jesus, he advised her that he needed to ascend to the Father, and that she should advise the disciples, which she did. Later that day Jesus appeared before the disciples, except for Thomas. According to John Jesus performed many signs before his disciples that had not been written (John 19:38-21:19).

Though written some 60 years after Jesus resurrection and appearances, the writer of John is claiming dictation by an unknown disciple allegedly beloved by Jesus. Some scholars believe that John originally ended with Chapter 20, as quoted below.

> Now Jesus did many other signs in the presence of his disciples, which are not written in this book. But these are written so that you may come to believe that Jesus is the Messiah, the Son of God, and that through believing you may have life in his name (John 20:30-31).

At the end of the current version of John, after Jesus' resurrection and appearance, Jesus asks Peter to follow him, and Peter says, *"Lord, what about him?"* referring to an unnamed disciple. Jesus says, *"If it is my will that he remain until I come, what is that to you?"* (John 21:20-23). In closing, the writer of John says:

> This is the disciple who is testifying to these things and has written them, and we know that his testimony is true. But there are also many other things that Jesus did; if every one of them were written down, I suppose that the world itself could not contain the books that would be written (John 21:24).

It would appear that the writer of John realized John was offering a different message about Jesus and Jesus' nature than the three synoptic gospels that preceded John. The writer of John appears to be claiming a unique basis for the significant factual and theological differences from the three synoptic gospels.

The Jefferson Bible

President, Thomas Jefferson, created his own version of the New Testament by cutting and pasting excerpts from the Gospels of Matthew, Mark, Luke and John. What has become known as the *Jefferson Bible* included Jesus' teachings and parables, but omitted various healings, miracles and the resurrection. Jefferson never called what he created a bible, and he never published it. It remained a part of his private writings. The source for a letter transmitting Jefferson's Bible, set forth below, that included the last two paragraphs, was lost to this author when needed for purposes of citation and attribution.

> Like Socrates and Epictetus, [Jesus] wrote nothing himself. But he had not, like them, a Xenophon or an Arian to write for him.... On the contrary, all the learned in his country, entrenched in its power and riches, were opposed to him, lest his labors should undermine their advantages; and the committing of his life and doctrine fell on unlettered and ignorant men; who wrote, too, from memory, and not till long after the transaction had passed.

> According to the ordinary fate of those who attempt to enlighten and reform mankind, He fell an early victim to the jealousy and combination of the alter and the throne, at about 33 years of age, his reason having not yet attained the maximum of its energy, nor the course of preaching, which was but of three years at most, presented occasions for developing a complete system of morals. Hence the doctrines which he really delivered were defective, as a whole, and fragments only of what he did deliver have come to us mutilated, and often unintelligible.

> They have been still more disfigured by the corruptions of schematizing followers, who have found an interest in sophisticating and perverting the simple doctrine he taught, by engrafting on them the mysticisms of a Grecian Sophist (Plato), frittering them into subtitles and obscuring them with jargon, until they have caused good men to reject the whole in disgust, and to view Jesus as an imposter...

Notwithstanding these disadvantages, a system of morals is presented to us which, if filled up in the true style and spirit of the rich fragments he left us, would be the most perfect and sublime that has ever been taught to man. The question of his being a member of the Godhead, or in direct communication with it, claimed for him by some of his followers, and denied by others, is foreign to the present view...

His moral doctrines, relating to kindred and friends, were more pure and perfect than those of the most correct of the philosophers...and they went far beyond both in inculcating universal philanthropy, not only to kindred and friends, to neighbors and countrymen, but to all mankind, gathering all into one family, under the bonds of love, charity, peace, common wants and common aids. A development of this head will evince the peculiar superiority of the system of Jesus over all others...

He pushed his scrutinies into the heart of man; erected his tribunal in the region of thought, and purified the waters of the fountainhead. He taught emphatically the doctrine of a future state, which was either doubted or disbelieved by the Jews; and wielded it with efficacy as an important incentive, supplementary to the other motives to moral conduct.

I too have made a wee-little book from [the Gospels] which I call the Philosophy of Jesus. It is a paradigm of his doctrines made by cutting the texts out of the book and arranging them on the pages of a blank book.... A more beautiful or precious a morsel of ethics I have never seen.... I am a disciple of the doctrines of Jesus, very different from the Platonists...who draw all their characteristic dogmas from what its author never said nor saw. They have compounded from the heathen mysteries a system beyond the comprehension of man of which [Jesus], were he to return to earth, would not recognize one feature.

In the Beginning: Bibles Before the Year 1,000

The Smithsonian Sackler Museum exhibition in Washington, D.C., *"In the Beginning: Bibles Before the Year 1,000,"* was on display from October 21, 2006 through January 7, 2007. Alan Cooperman, a *Washington Post* Staff Writer at the time, wrote a narrative of the exhibit. He stated:

> These are documents with the proven power to shake faith. That's what happened to Bart D. Ehrman, author of his 2005 bestseller "Misquoting Jesus: The Story Behind Who Changed the Bible and Why." Ehrman was a born-again Christian from Kansas when he entered Chicago's Moody Bible Institute at age 18. After three decades of comparing ancient manuscripts in their original languages to try to determine the earliest, most authentic text of the New Testament, he is now an agnostic. *"I thought God had inspired the words inerrantly. But when I examined the historical texts, I realized the words had not been preserved inerrantly, and it would have been no greater miracle to preserve them than to inspire them in the first place,"* said Ehrman, now chairman of religious studies at the University of North Carolina at Chapel Hill.

Among the writings that ultimately were not accepted into the Christian Canon, the Sackler shows a 2nd century fragment of the Unknown Gospel, which includes a story of an attempt to stone Jesus, and a 3rd century papyrus known as the Sayings of

Jesus, including this one: Jesus says: "*A prophet is not acceptable in his own country, nor does a physician work cures on those who know him.*"

As Christians were establishing what was in and what was out, they began compiling the New Testament in a book, or codex. In the physical and ideological heart of the exhibition are two stained parchment pages of a meticulous Greek script from one of the most celebrated: Codex Sinaiticus, discovered in 1859 at St. Catherine's Monastery in the Sinai Desert.

Ever since it came to light, Sinaiticus has been a pivotal document—and a theological challenge—for scholars like Ehrman. Together with a few other documents, it forms the basis for the most authoritative modern versions of the Old Testament in the original Greek.

Ehrman noted that its version of the Gospel of John is missing the story of the woman taken in adultery, the famous parable in which Jesus says to those who would kill the woman, "Let the one among you who is without sin cast the first stone." [Ehrman] and many other textual scholars believe the adultery story was not introduced into John until the Middle Ages…

There was much more to the Exhibit. However, the Exhibit simply served to show that the scraps and fragments of the earliest manuscripts in existence do not reflect today's biblical versions. Unfortunately, the inerrant word of God no longer exists.

Today's Bibles: Inerrancy

A number of discrepancies and inconsistencies were noted in the biblical texts and narrations earlier in this chapter. There is also at times a tying together of what were separate and different stories or narratives, written by different authors at different times. For example, in

Genesis 1:9-27, God created vegetation on the third day, sea life and land animals on the fourth and fifth days, and then male and female humans simultaneously on the sixth day. The female was created as a part of humankind, not from Adam's rib. God told them to be fruitful and multiply, giving them dominion over the fruit of every tree to eat without restriction, and dominion over all the Earth (Genesis 1:28-29).

In Genesis 2:4–3:24, God first created man before plant life, and admonished him not to eat from the tree of knowledge of good and evil, or he would die. Woman was then created out of the man's rib. Woman already knew not to eat from the tree of knowledge. The land of Eden, by the Tigris and the Euphrates rivers (Genesis 2:13-14), is in Babylon where the Israelites were in captivity when this story was probably written, during the sixth century BCE. God put man in the Garden of Eden to till it and keep it. There is no mention of man's dominion over all the earth. Man and woman, named Adam and Eve, were forbidden from eating from the tree of knowledge.

In the story of the flood God instructs Noah to board the animals two by two. The animals are boarded two by two, irrespective of whether they were clean or unclean (Genesis 6:19, 7:8-9, 15). However, in Genesis 7:2, God's instructions are to board clean animals and birds of the air seven by seven, and animals that are not clean two by two. While this could be a reference to the clean and unclean foods, the concept of clean and unclean foods is not introduced until the much later time of Moses (Leviticus 11).

Different versions of an event by two authors are encountered. The first meeting of David and King Saul occurs when Jesse's son, David, as a harp player, is brought to King Saul's house to play his harp to comfort King Saul's malady (1 Samuel 16:17-23). Later, Saul meets David again just before the battle between David and Goliath where Saul doesn't know David, or Jesse, his father (1 Samuel 17:55-58). In one biblical account David slays Goliath (1 Samuel 17:48-51). In other biblical accounts Elhanan slays Goliath (2 Samuel 21:19), and Goliath's brother (1 Chronicles 20:5).

Jerome (CE 345–420) was a Roman, a devout believer, and a brilliant and meticulous scholar. He worked in a Bethlehem monastery during the Roman Empire for the last 30 years of his life creating a Latin translation of the books that became today's Bible from versions of ancient Hebrew and Greek Old Testament, and Greek New Testament manuscripts. His translation became the standard Christian Bible for the next 1,100 years. In his letters he stated:

> I am not so stupid as to think that any of the Lord's words either need correcting or are not divinely inspired; but the Latin manuscripts of the Scriptures are proved faulty by the variations which are found in all of them.

Jerome, in describing the appearance of Moses in Exodus 34:29, translated the Hebrew word for *"rays of light"* to horns. The word for *"rays of light"* can be understood as horns in a different context. Thus, Jerome's version of the Bible had Moses coming down from Sinai with horns on his head. Michelangelo's statue of Moses erected in 1545 in St. Peter's Cathedral in Rome, relying on the biblical description of Moses having horns, depicts Moses with horns. Modern Bibles state that Moses' face was shining, rather than describing Moses as having horns.

In today's world we have Jews who use a different order and set of books for their Torah than what appears as the Old Testament for Christians. We have hundreds of millions of Roman Catholic Christians who rely on different books in their Bible than Protestant Christians, and Eastern Orthodox Christians who include still other books, not included by Roman Catholics or Protestants.

The Roman Catholic Bible includes seven books not in the Protestant Bible: Tobit, Judith, and 1 and 2 Maccabees, Wisdom and Sirach

(Ecclesiasticus), and Baruch. The Greek Orthodox Bible includes all the books in the Roman Catholic Bible, but adds Psalm 151 (Psalm of David when he slew Goliath), 3 Maccabees and the letter of Manasseh. There is a 4 Maccabees that is included in the appendix to the Greek Bible. The Prayer of Manasseh and Psalm 151 were included in the Vulgate version of the Roman Catholic Bible, but not in present day versions. Not all the books that appear are identical. The Roman Catholic and Greek Orthodox versions of Esther include 103 versus not included in the Protestant version. There are other differences in the order and content.

Paul warns that Jesus will not return until *"He [the lawless one] opposes and exalts himself above every so-called god or object of worship, so that he takes his seat in the temple of God, declaring himself to be God."* (2 Thessalonians 2:4). 2nd Thessalonians was written sometime during 50-51 CE, before the temple was destroyed by the Romans in 70 CE. Paul died about 64 CE never knowing the temple would be destroyed. The temple was used for animal sacrifices that could no longer be practiced after the temple was destroyed. For the biblical literalist, 2 Thessalonians requires the temple as a condition precedent to the Jesus' return.

John was written after the temple was destroyed. John describes Jesus as stating that if the temple were destroyed, Jesus would rebuild it in three days. John was referring to Jesus speaking of the temple as his body (John 2:19-22). John's portrayal of the temple as Jesus' body being resurrected, after the temple was destroyed, obviates Paul's 2nd Thessalonians requirement that a temple exist as a condition for Jesus' return. Believers of the Bible as the inerrant word of God might argue against that conclusion, and take measures to accelerate the result, though Paul considers God to dwell in the temple of the body (1 Corinthians 3:16, 6:19). Believers that the Bible is the inerrant word of God will continue to believe in inerrancy, notwithstanding the evidence to the contrary. Relying on the Bible to predict future events is equally problematic.

Believers that the Bible is the literal, inerrant word of God will also continue to believe that the earth is only six thousand years old and that dinosaurs roamed the earth during Jesus' lifetime. The Aristotle, Greco-Roman view in Jesus' time was that the earth was flat and that the stars and planets revolved around it. As late as 1633 Galileo was subjected to a church inquisition for his heliocentric heresy that the earth and planets revolved around the sun.

Chapter 2.

THE APOSTLE PAUL AND ACTS

As stated above, Jesus' death and resurrection are believed to have occurred about 30 CE. We know about the Apostle Paul through Acts of the Apostles and through the letters Paul wrote. Paul's letters were written from about 50 CE through 64 CE. His first letter to the Thessalonians was written about 50 CE, two decades after Jesus' resurrection. Acts was written by the same author as the Gospel of Luke, sometime after 85 CE. Acts, like Luke, is dedicated to the unknown person named Theophilus. Acts begins with a recapitulation of Jesus' appearances to his disciples, the baptism of the disciples with the Holy Spirit, and Jesus' ascension into heaven after 40 days. Though the writer of Luke also wrote Acts, Acts is the only biblical writing about Jesus' post resurrection appearances that has Jesus remaining on earth for 40 days after his resurrection. Acts is the only biblical writing indicating the apostles would be blessed by Jesus with the Holy Spirit. Acts is the only biblical writing describing the disciples performing miracles.

Acts has Peter and other disciples spreading the word about Jesus, and performing wonders and signs in Jerusalem. They are pressured, threatened and flogged for doing so by the Jewish authorities. Ultimately, they prevail because of their faith and fearlessness. Acts includes descriptions of the resistance to the activities of Peter, John and their followers by Jews who were not followers of Jesus. This resistance included the stoning and martyrdom of Stephen at the behest of Paul before Paul's conversion to become an advocate for Jesus, and others who considered Stephen's beliefs to have been blasphemous (Acts 7:1–8:1).

As portrayed in Acts Paul was raised a Jew, a Pharisee, who vigorously persecuted the early followers of Jesus. According to Acts, Paul's conversion to becoming an advocate for Jesus occurred while Paul was traveling to Damascus to prosecute Jews who had become followers there. This occurred an undetermined time after Jesus' resurrection and appearances to his disciples. According to Acts, Paul was blinded by a great light from heaven. He heard Jesus' voice instructing him to continue to Damascus to receive further instructions. The men allegedly traveling with Paul heard the voice but saw no one. After arriving in Damascus, Paul regained his sight when a disciple, Ananias, laid his hands on him based on Jesus' instructions (Acts 9:1-19).

In a second Acts account of Paul's conversion, the men traveling with Paul saw the light but did not hear the voice, unlike the first account (Acts 22:9). After his conversion, Paul was with disciples in Damascus and began to proclaim Jesus in the synagogues. According to Acts, Paul returned to Jerusalem. Though the apostles in Jerusalem were concerned when Paul appeared, after Barnabas described to the apostles that Paul had accepted Jesus, Paul was able to move among them. Paul left for Tarsus because he was in danger. Acts is unclear as to when Paul first visited Jerusalem, but infers Paul went very soon after his conversion (Acts 9:19-30).

In the meantime, Acts describes a vision by Peter in which he refuses to eat food he considered unclean. However, a voice from heaven allegedly convinced him that *"what God had made clean, you shall not profane"*. Peter allegedly became convinced that the Holy Spirit had been poured out to the Gentiles as well as the Jews (Acts 10:1-48). Though the disciples were initially skeptical, Peter allegedly convinced them and believers in Judea that the Holy Spirit was made available to the Gentiles (Acts11:1-18).

Though it is unclear when Paul first visited Jerusalem, Paul was allegedly welcomed by the church, the apostles, and the elders. Some believers in the church claimed it was necessary for Paul's followers to be circumcised and keep the Law of Moses to become true followers of Jesus. Peter and James allegedly spoke up on behalf of Paul, stating Paul's ministry to the Gentiles did not require compliance with the Laws of Moses. Peters' and James' followers then allegedly agreed (Acts 15:1-21).

The writer of Acts, writing three or more decades after Paul's letters, must have been aware of Paul's letters, particularly since so much of Acts is about Paul. However, Paul specifically states that after his conversion he did not confer with disciples or anyone, and did not go to Jerusalem, but went to Arabia and then returned to Damascus (Galatians 1:15-17). By Paul's own account he did not go to Jerusalem until three years after his conversion, when he stayed with Peter for 15 days. At that time Paul stated that besides Peter, he saw none of the Apostles except for James, Jesus' brother (Galatians 1:15-19). By Paul's own account, for three years after his conversion before he conferred with the Jesus' disciples, Paul became an advocate for Jesus without consulting about his advocacy with any of Jesus' followers in Jerusalem.

Paul describes his own conversion as occurring after Jesus appeared to Peter, then to the twelve, then to more than 500, most of whom were still alive, then to James and the apostles, and lastly to Paul (1

Corinthians 15:5–8). There is no mention of Jesus appearing to the 500 other than by Paul. Jesus consistently appears to "the eleven", meaning the twelve apostles minus Judas who had betrayed Jesus and ended up taking his own life. Only Paul has Jesus appearing to the twelve, perhaps because Paul was unaware of Judas' betrayal of Jesus. Paul relates no incidence of blindness in his letters. Though the gospels had not been written when Paul wrote his letters, there were oral traditions about Jesus that could explain Paul's knowledge of Jesus, though not the discrepancies noted. Paul proclaimed that just as Peter was entrusted with the gospel for the circumcised, Jesus entrusted Paul with the gospel for the uncircumcised (Galatians, 2:7-9). However, Jesus' mission for Paul included bringing Jesus' message to the Jews (Acts 9:15).

In some respects Paul's conversion experience as described in Acts was not unlike that of Joseph Smith, Jr., the founder of the Church of Jesus Christ of Latter Day Saints. Smith claimed he saw a series of visions, later described as God and Jesus that directed him to a buried book of golden plates. Smith published an English translation of those plates that is called the Book of Mormon. His followers consider the revelations in the Book of Mormon to be scripture. His followers regard him as a prophet comparable to Moses.

Paul is generally credited with writing the following 13 letters that were ultimately incorporated into the New Testament: Romans, 1 and 2 Corinthians, Galatians, Ephesians, Philippians, Colossians, 1 and 2 Thessalonians, 1 and 2 Timothy, Titus and Philemon. Though the letter to the Hebrews was originally thought to have been written by Paul, biblical scholars have concluded that Paul did not write Hebrews. Its author remains unknown.

There is scholarly doubt and debate that Paul wrote 1 and 2 Timothy, Titus, Ephesians, Colossians and 2 Thessalonians. The reasons vary. One reason for doubt is because of an apparent inconsistency in Paul's views on slavery and bondage. In Philemon 1:8-18, Paul advocates release of a slave. Yet Paul endorses slavery in Colossians 3:22–4:1, Ephesians 6:5-9 and Titus 2:9-10. Some evaluate differences in writing style and word usage. Others note that the church structure was not as well developed in Paul's time as the references to church structure in 1 and 2 Timothy and Titus. Paul's writing Colossians is doubted, because it counters Gnostic beliefs that allegedly didn't exist until the second century, long after Paul died. Inconsistencies between Paul's letters and Acts are also cited. There was a 3 Corinthians referred to in ancient literature that was rejected for inclusion in the Bible as a forgery.

There are several of Paul's writings that he mentions in his letters that have been lost. These include a letter to the Corinthians mentioned in 1 Corinthians 5:9, a letter to the Corinthians mentioned in 2 Corinthians 2:4 and 7:8-9, a letter to the Ephesians mentioned in Ephesians 3:2-4, and a letter from Laodicea mentioned in Colossians 4:16. For purposes of this book all of Paul's 13 letters are considered as written by Paul.

Paul's message to the Gentiles had little to do with Jesus' message conveying God's ministry and requirements for achieving the kingdom of heaven. Paul's message was more about Jesus himself. Paul's message was that because of Adam's disobedience of God in eating from the tree of knowledge, humans were incapable of living without sin. Thus, it was only faith and belief in Jesus' crucifixion and resurrection that insured everlasting life, because Jesus allegedly died for the forgiveness of sins (Genesis 3:11-19, Romans 5:12-21, 1 Corinthians 15:22). This issue, now known as *"original sin"* is discussed in Chapter 3. Paul's views that salvation is assured through acceptance of Jesus as Lord and Savior are consistent with Paul's belief in a resurrection as a Pharisee, but inconsistent with Jesus' ministry as expressed in the synoptic gospels of Mark, Matthew and Luke, the Letter of James, and in Paul's statements relating to his beliefs in predestination. See Chapter 5, THE REFORMATION: JUSTIFICATION BY FAITH ALONE: PREDESTINATION.

Paul preached that belief in Jesus as Lord and Savior supplanted the Law of Moses (Romans 7:4-6, Galatians 3:13-14, 23-27, 5:4, Ephesians 2:15). Paul also preached that, *"a person is not justified by the works of the Law, but by faith in Jesus Christ"* (Galatians 2:16). As stated above, Paul's beliefs that works were no longer needed to comply with the law and that Jesus came to supplant the law, specifically conflict with the beliefs about Jesus as set forth in the Gospel of Matthew and in the Letter of James.

Jesus states in the gospel of Matthew:

> Do not think that I have come to abolish the law or the prophets; I have come not to abolish but to fulfill. For truly I tell you, until heaven and earth pass away, not one letter, not one stroke of a letter, will pass from the law until all is accomplished (Matthew 5:17-18).

James states that faith without works is dead (James 2:26).

Before and after visiting Jerusalem, Paul went on his way preaching and converting Gentiles throughout Asia Minor and its environs. However, when Peter was in Antioch, Peter refused to eat with the Gentiles after disciples of James had spoken to Peter. Some Galatians had apparently recanted their affiliation with Paul in favor of becoming followers of Peter and James. Paul's view of Peter's actions angered Paul and indicated that, contrary to Acts, no agreement allowing Paul to preach his message to the Gentiles came into being. Paul's statement in Galatians 2:9-14 is quoted below:

> But when Peter came to Antioch, I opposed him to his face, because he stood self-condemned; for until certain people came from James he used to eat with the gentiles. But after they came he drew back and kept himself separate for fear of the circumcision faction. And the other Jews joined him in his hypocrisy, so that even Barnabas was led astray by their hypocrisy. But when

I saw that they were not acting consistently with the truth of the gospel, I said to Peter before them all, "If you, though a Jew, live like a Gentile and not like a Jew, how can you compel the gentiles to live like Jews?

The gospel Paul referred to in Galatians was Paul's interpretation of his mission to the Gentiles. The New Testament Gospels had not been written and Paul did not support his mission to the Gentiles by reference to the Torah (Galatians 1:11-12). Paul attempted to convince the allegedly wayward Galatians that they were wrong in rejecting Paul's ministry (Galatians 2:11, 6:18). Peter, for his part, had unspecified issues with Paul's beliefs as expressed in unidentified letters of Paul:

So also our beloved brother Paul, wrote to you according to the wisdom given him, speaking of this [living perfectly] as he does in all his letters. There are some things in them hard to understand, which the ignorant and unstable twist to their own destruction, as they do the other scriptures. You therefore, beloved, since you are forewarned beware that you are not carried away with the error of the lawless and lose your own stability. (2 Peter 3:15-17).

Peter, writing to the exiles in the Dispersion of Pontus, Galatia, Cappadocia, Asia and Bithynia, warned them to live not by their desires, but by God's will, since they had already spent enough time behaving as the Gentiles living their lives in licentiousness, passions, drunkenness, carousing and lawless idolatry (1 Peter 4:3). Peter, in writing to the Dispersion was writing to the Gentiles who had become followers of Jesus. Peter throughout his message emphasized living by God's will as conveyed by Jesus' teachings. Though not specifically stated, living by Jesus' teachings was not simply accepting Jesus as Lord and Savior for the forgiveness of their sins.

Acts refers to as many as five unspecified trips by Paul to Jerusalem that are not corroborated in Paul's letters (Acts 9:26-27, 11:29-30, 15:1-19, 18:21-22, 21:17 and 24:17). Paul mentions the trip 3 years after his conversions, again 14 years after, and a visit at an unspecified time which could be a reference to one of the previous two trips (Galatians 1:17-18, 2:1-10 and Romans 21:17). According to Paul, after his first visit, he returned again to Jerusalem after 14 years, taking Barnabas and Titus with him. At this time he described to *"acknowledged leaders"* of the church what he had been preaching to convert Gentiles to become followers of Jesus. Neither Peter nor James was present at the time. It's possible that both had been killed. The acknowledged leaders with whom Paul spoke remained antagonistic towards Paul's views. Paul stated *"those leaders contributed nothing to me"* (Galatians 2:1-6). Paul advised these leaders that Peter, James and John, had recognized the grace given to Paul. These leaders then agreed that Paul could preach to the Gentiles, though Paul was always to remember the poor (Galatians 2:7-9).

While in Jerusalem, Paul was accosted by Sadducees who brought him before a council with the intent of killing him, because of his preaching on behalf of Jesus. Paul noticed that there were also Pharisees in the group accusing him. He called out that he was a Pharisee on trial for his belief in the resurrection of the dead. The Pharisees believed in the resurrection of the dead. The Sadducees did not. The Pharisees in the group accusing Paul interceded on his behalf, and the threat to his life ended, at least temporarily (Acts 23:1-9).

Paul's belief in the resurrection of the dead as a Pharisee was consistent with his preaching that resurrection and an afterlife could be achieved by accepting Jesus as Lord and Savior. Paul never identified the basis for his belief in a resurrection as a Pharisee. Whatever that basis was, Paul apparently changed his beliefs to thinking that Jesus' resurrection made it possible for Gentiles and all Jews to be resurrected by belief in Jesus as Lord and Savior, not only Pharisees. Paul was tried by Roman authorities in Jerusalem at the behest of his Jewish accusers (Acts 25:1-5). After describing his vision and conversion, his Roman advocate exclaimed that Paul was out of his mind from too much learning (Acts 26:24-25). Ultimately, Paul was released notwithstanding his Jewish accusers on the basis that he had done nothing to warrant imprisonment or death by the Roman authorities (Acts 26:30-32).

After this trial and release he sailed to Rome. Paul was imprisoned in Rome as a Roman citizen. The Roman authorities were willing to release him, but did not do so because of Jewish opposition that required an appeal to the emperor. On appeal the authorities wanted to hear from Paul stating, *"We would like to hear from you what you think, for with regard to this sect we know that everywhere it is spoken against"* (Acts 28:21-22). Paul's explanation as an advocate of Jesus did not convince the authorities to release him.

Acts ends after Paul had been imprisoned in Rome for two years (Acts 28:30-31). Paul's death and alleged martyrdom occurred as a result of Emperor Nero by many experts' accounts between 64 and 66 CE. Historical records indicate that a significant fire occurred in Rome in July of 64 CE; destroying much of the city. Rumors arose that Nero had intentionally set the fire. Nero blamed the Christians for the fire in order to deflect the rumors. Many Christians were rounded up and subjected to persecution, torture and death. These persecutions might have resulted in Peter's death. Paul is thought to have at least temporarily survived them because of his Roman citizenship.

Significantly, the synoptic gospels of Mark, Matthew and Luke were written after Paul's letters. The writers of these gospels surely had heard of Paul's travels and ministry. Though the three synoptic gospels tend to corroborate each other, none mentions Paul's letters or specifically advocates Paul's beliefs or ministry. The synoptic gospels reflected oral traditions originating with Jesus' ministry. Jesus' ministry emphasized loving our neighbors as ourselves, living by the golden rule, being magnanimous to those who ask of us, caring about the poor, the afflicted, the imprisoned, by acting and giving, not just remuneration from our abundance, but giving time, effort and love with self-sacrifice, to those from whom no love, return or remuneration is sought, quietly and without notoriety. The three synoptic gospels' silence about Paul's mission and ministry is an implicit rejection of Paul's mission and ministry.

The author of Luke in the later written Acts attempts to meld Paul's ministry with the ministry of Jesus' disciples. The evidence is mixed as to how much of an agreement occurred with Jesus' disciples in the Jerusalem church, and how widely any such agreement was accepted. Jesus' ministry did not include worshipping Jesus as Lord and Savior. Jesus achieved immortality by conveying God's message for achieving the kingdom of heaven, by his exemplary life devoted to God, and by his obedience to God until the very end. Nevertheless, the Nicene form of Christianity developed by the Greek and Roman Gentiles of the Church in Rome, and preached by today's churches, gives Paul's message and ministry that Jesus overcame Adam's sin, precedence over Jesus' message and ministry. It also deifies Jesus to a status he never claimed.

Chapter 3.

ORIGINAL SIN

The Apostle Paul originated the concept of original sin through the letters he wrote, though he didn't use that term. Irenaeus, the bishop of Lyon, and St. Augustine, of Hippo, developed the concept during the first four centuries, based on Paul's letters. Paul believed that Adam's sin of disobeying God by eating from the tree of knowledge permeated all the unborn and all future generations with sin. Based on Adam's disobedience, Paul preached that humans were incapable of saving themselves from disobedience to God, and that acceptance of Jesus' sacrifice on the cross was needed for their salvation (Genesis 3:11-19, Romans 5:12-21, 1 Corinthians 15:22). In a nutshell Paul stated that *"Just as one man's trespass led to condemnation for all, so one man's act of righteousness leads to justification and life for all"* (Romans 5:18).

To begin with, the concept of original sin was unknown to ancient Judaism in Jesus' time. *"God saw everything that he had made* [including male and female created in his image], *and indeed, it was very good*" (Genesis 1:31). Significantly, as set forth in the previous chapter, Paul as a Pharisee already believed in the resurrection of the dead, and used this fact to extricate himself from a trial for his beliefs (Act 23:1-9).

Contrary to Paul's preaching, scripture does not provide that Adam's disobedience resulted in human mortality, or that inherent sinfulness is transmitted forever into perpetuity throughout humanity. Indeed, long after Adam, and before Jesus, God in preaching the Ten Commandments and other laws to Moses preached as though the ancient Israelites could obey and achieve what was being preached, not that they would fail as Paul's beliefs require. Moses, in preaching God's word to his people stated: *"Surely this commandment that I am commanding you today is not too hard for you, nor is it too far away....No, the word is very near to you; it is in your mouth and in your heart for you to observe"* (Deuteronomy 30:11-14). Thus, long after Adam, and contrary to what Paul preached, scripture provided that the ancient Israelites were capable of following the Law.

Significantly, Jesus, speaking about those considered worthy in the Old Testament stated:

> Indeed they cannot die anymore, because they are like angels and children of God, being children of the resurrection. And the fact that the dead are raised Moses himself showed in the story about the bush, where he speaks of the Lord as the God of Abraham, the God of Isaac, and the God of Jacob. Now he is God not of the dead but of the living; for to him all of them are alive (Luke 20:36-38).

Further, before Jesus, the prospective mother and father of John the Baptist were both *"righteous before God, living blamelessly according to all the commandments and regulations of the Lord"* (Luke 1:6). John the Baptist was a righteous and holy man who was regarded as a prophet (Mark 6:20, Matthew 14:5). Mary, mother of Jesus, found favor with God (Luke 1:30). Well before Jesus and contrary to Paul's original sin theory Noah (2 Peter 2:5), Abraham, David, Job, Moses, Elijah (2 Kings 2:11-13) and other Old Testament persons were found to be in great favor by God. Enoch had pleased God and was taken by God without experiencing death (Genesis 5:24, Hebrews 11:5).

Aside from the fact that humanity had not been burdened with original sin as Paul preached, scripture indicates human mortality did not arise from Adam's disobedience. God's punishment for Adam's eating from the tree of knowledge was not death, but a life of hard work until his return to dust. For Eve the punishment was increased pain in childbearing (Genesis 3:16-19). Thus, Adam and Eve were already mortal beings. This is further clarified because God banished Adam and Eve from the Garden of Eden so that they would not eat of the tree of life, not because they had eaten from the tree of knowledge. Eating from the tree of life would allow Adam and Eve to become immortal like the gods (Genesis 3:22-24). Thus, God never created Adam or humankind to be immortal.

Reaching back to the Old Testament, King David's Psalm 51:4-5, while sometimes cited in support of original sin, actually has the opposite effect in its proper context. Psalm 51:4-5 states that, *"Against you, you alone have I sinned [with Bathsheba] and done what is evil in your sight, so that you are justified in your sentence and blameless when you pass judgment. Indeed I was born guilty, a sinner when my mother conceived me."*

David acknowledged his sin and asked for God's forgiveness. Judaism did not recognize the concept of original sin, and David's reference to his being a sinner when conceived is indicative of the degree to which he was contrite in his confession of guilt. Contrary to Paul, David's transgression against God did not preclude him from receiving God's blessing and salvation. God's forgiveness and salvation was precisely what David was praying for. David was not praying in vain. Indeed, the Lord speaking of David stated, *"Your house and your kingdom shall be made sure forever before me, your throne shall be established forever"* (2 Samuel 7:16).

Pelagius (360-418) was learned in Christian theology, fluent in Greek and Latin, and became well known throughout the Roman Empire. Pelagius was wrongly accused by St. Augustine and others of denying the need for grace in the performance of works needed to perfect faith. He was accused of being a heretic, and consequently, virtually none of his writing has survived. Pelagius' Commentary on Romans as set forth in Google Docs is a writing that did survive. Most of what is known about him is derived from the writings of his accusers including St. Augustine who had close political access to Pope Innocent I for purposes of castigating and condemning Pelagius.

Before their dispute regarding original sin, St. Augustine, a pillar of the church at the time, but a believer in Manichaeism previously, declared Pelagius to be a saintly man. Pelagius lectured that humans were not destined for death because of Adam's sin. He believed that children were not born with sin and are not put to death for the sins and transgressions of their parents, as original sin requires, but only for their own sins and transgressions, relying on Deuteronomy 24:16. The Deuteronomy relied upon by Pelagius cannot be lightly dismissed, since it is one of the commandments given by God to Moses. Deuteronomy 24:16 states:

> Parents shall not be put to death for their children, nor shall children be put to death for their parents; only for their own crimes may persons be put to death.

Further, Pelagius and his followers also relied on Luke 20:36-38, where as stated above, Jesus, speaking of those considered worthy in the Old Testament stated:

Indeed they cannot die anymore, because they are like angels and children of God, being children of the resurrection. And the fact that the dead are raised Moses himself showed, in the story about the bush, where he speaks of the Lord as the God of Abraham, the God of Isaac, and the God of Jacob. Now he is God not of the dead but of the living; for to him all of them are alive.

Thus, contrary to Paul, persons found favor with God long before Jesus' ministry, crucifixion and resurrection, as did Paul as a Pharisee. Though the original sin theory is not necessarily invalidated by the undesirable results of its application, it does produce undesirable results. For example, if a newborn dies prior to baptism, the newborn is not saved because the newborn was born with original sin. The infant would find itself in hell, in some level of Dante's Inferno, or in the Roman Catholicism's later developed concept of Purgatory.

Jesus' obedience to God and his ministry is exemplified by scripture that indicates that Jesus was fearful and overcome at Gethsemane when confronted with facing his destiny. Jesus knew he was facing betrayal, trial, crucifixion and death. He asked God that if it were possible, to let the cup pass from him; but that it should not be what [Jesus] wanted, but what God wanted (Matthew 26:36-46, Luke 22:39-46). Jesus bowed to God's will and went through with his arrest, trial, crucifixion and death. Jesus offered prayers and supplications, with loud cries and tears to the one who was able to save him from his death, (Hebrews 5:7). He cried out on the cross asking why God had forsaken him (Mark 15:34, Matthew 27:45-50).

God resurrected Jesus because of his exemplary life and his obedience to God until the very end, not because of Adam's sin. Original sin played no role in Jesus' ministry, crucifixion and resurrection. Jesus faithfully conveyed God's message to humanity that the kingdom of heaven could be achieved by living in accordance with God's word.

Jesus led an exemplary life by resisting the temptations of evil and devoting his life to conveying God's message. Jesus earned his status as Son and eternal life by his faith and obedience to God until the very end, not because Adam and Eve ate from the forbidden tree of knowledge.

Chapter 4.

THE HISTORICAL CONTEXT
OF THE GOSPEL OF JOHN

The Gospel of John was written about 95 CE. The writer or writers of John had the difficult task of reconstructing the events that occurred 65 years earlier. It would be similar to a writer in 2015 describing the Korean War; General MacArthur's being fired by President Truman; the conviction and execution of the Ethel and Julius Rosenberg for treason; or the 1953 CIA sponsored coup returning the Shah of Iran to power. There were no printing presses, photos, radio, television, internet or recorded history during the 65 years in issue.

Paul's letters, the Gospels of Mark, Matthew and Luke, and the book of Acts had all been written by the time John was written. However, John is very much an original work, not relying much on the writings that preceded it. John does not reconstruct the events that occurred 65 years earlier. John reinterprets those events and casts them in a light that, in many respects, is inconsistent and contradictory to the synoptic gospels.

Unlike Peter, Paul and Jesus' other disciples, when John was written, the writer of John had the benefit of knowing that Jesus' return was not imminent. Further, neither Paul's nor Peter's ministries, the Jerusalem church, nor the synoptic gospels were successful in convincing the majority of Jews to be followers of Jesus. Finally, the destruction of the second Jewish temple in 70 CE, and the movement of Judaism from a sacrificial religion toward a Torah study religion finalized the long developing schism between Jewish followers of Jesus and those who were not. There are two issues with John that are discussed here; first, the statement in John 14:6, and second, the deification of Jesus. The political and historical context during which John was written are needed to place the Gospel of John in a proper perspective and limit its overriding importance and influence on present day Christianity.

No One Comes To The Father Except Through Me.

"I am the way, and the truth, and the life. No one comes to the Father except through me" (John 14:6).

A reading of the Plato-Socrates dialogues from the 4th Century BCE, indicates that Socrates lead a saintly existence; never striving for material wealth; living simply and in relative poverty; devoting his life to the understanding of truth, justice, beauty, the meaning of life; attempting to teach, transform and convert what he believed to be a corrupt and errant society; and ultimately paying with his life for his beliefs. Socrates, a Greek, lived centuries before Jesus and never followed the law. Socrates did not know Jesus. Like Jesus, Socrates remained silent at his trial before the Greek authorities who had condemned him to death. Thus, according to John, Socrates' contributions to the betterment and knowledge of humanity apparently will remain unrewarded except for his place in history. Perhaps for Socrates this is enough.

Many Christians, including Christian clergy, rely on John 14:6 to disparage other religions as false. However, when the historical context is known during which the Gospel of John was written, John 14:6 has a much more limited effect. The letter to the Hebrews was written explaining that God had made a new covenant with his chosen people; that Jesus was the true high priest; and that animal sacrifices were not required or needed. The letter to the Hebrews, the existence of the Jerusalem church and the case made by the Gospel of Matthew that Jesus was born in fulfillment of biblical prophecy were unconvincing to the large majority of Jews.

Deuteronomy 21:23, states that anyone hung from a tree is under God's curse. Thus, dying in the manner in which Jesus died was seen as a disgrace and a curse to Jews. To the Jewish society and hierarchy at the time, Jesus had none of the credentials of an assumed Messiah. Jews who were expecting a Messiah did not expect the Messiah to suffer and die. The Jewish Messiah was expected to possess great power and grandeur, like the proverbial King David. The Messiah would be able to defeat God's enemies and restore God's kingdom on Earth. Moreover, the large majority of Jesus' followers were Gentiles, which further alienated the establishment Jews from becoming followers of Jesus.

While Jesus' acceptance was flourishing with Gentiles in Syria and Asia Minor, notwithstanding the early success of the Jerusalem church depicted in Acts, there was considerable opposition to the Jerusalem church and to followers of Jesus by establishment Judaism. Further, the Jewish sects of the Zealots, Sicarii, and Fourth Philosophy were rebellious and were instrumental in the Jewish uprising against the Romans that began in 66 CE. They believed that God had given them the land upon which they lived and the authority over it. In putting down the rebellion in 70 CE the Romans destroyed the Temple in Jerusalem, which had been rebuilt about 516 BCE, after the Persians released the Jews from their Babylonian captivity.

The destruction of the temple had a very negative impact on the

Sadducees who were in the upper echelon of Jewish society and made up the Sanhedrin. They fulfilled political and religious roles that included maintaining the temple and administering the temple sacrifices. The Sadducees lost their purpose, influence and stature, and essentially ceased to exist.

The Pharisees, who kept the law and had conducted their ritualistic animal sacrifices in the temple in accordance with Mosaic Law, could no longer conduct their animal sacrifices. Judaism had to be reinvented and it essentially fell upon the Pharisees and their Torah study role to do so. The evolution of Judaism from a temple, animal-sacrificial religion, to a Torah-study religion accelerated. This resulted in the development of a Pharisaic orthodoxy and the purging of nonconforming beliefs and practices including the followers of Jesus.

The Council of Jamnia, theorized as having taken place about 90 CE, has been largely discredited as occurring in terms of the creation of a Jewish Canon. However, the prayer, *birkat haminim*, blessing or cursing heretics, was thought to have been formulated during this time. Except for a small group of Jewish followers of Jesus in the Jerusalem Church, and a subgroup mentioned above as the Ebionites, the establishment Judaism including the powerful Pharisees did not consider that the Messiah had come, and that certainly, Jesus was not the Messiah. During this time frame, the schism between Jews and Jewish and Gentile followers of Jesus became irreconcilably formalized and fixed. The larger majority of Jews were not followers of Jesus. They considered the Jewish followers of Jesus to be holding blasphemous and heretical beliefs.

The writers of John were not concerned with the then still very popular contemporary gods of the Canaanites, Greeks, Romans or Egyptians with which they were very likely to have been aware of. It is not known if the writers of John were aware of or understood the eastern religions of Hinduism or Buddhism that existed at the time, though they were educated Gentiles; probably Greeks. The writers of John 14:6 focused their gospel message on the Jews who were not followers of Jesus. *"I am the way, and the truth, and the life. No one comes to the Father except through me,"* was directed to Jews who were not followers of Jesus. There is no indication that the writer or writers of John ever considered religions other than Judaism.

Paul's views on Jews who do not accept Jesus as their Lord and Savior are expressed in Romans 11:1, *"I ask, then, has God rejected his people? By no means! I myself am an Israelite, a descendent of Abraham."* And in Romans 11:25-26 Paul states: *"So that you may not claim to be wiser than you are, brothers and sisters, I want you to understand this mystery: a hardening has come upon part of Israel, until the full number of gentiles has come in. And so all of Israel will be saved; as it is written, 'Out of Zion will come the Deliverer.'"* Paul says *"for the gifts and the calling of God are irrevocable"* (Romans 11:29).

The Gospel of John concept of Jesus being with God from the beginning of time, and Jesus as God, would have been radical concepts even for Paul, and the writer of Matthew with their Jewish backgrounds, and the other synoptic gospel writers to accept. However, at the time John was written the large majority of Jesus' followers were Gentiles. Most probably the writer of John was also a Gentile, and the community in which John was written was most probably Gentile Greeks who became devoted followers of Jesus. Another possibility is that the community in which John was written was a Hellenist community. Hellenists were Jews outside Jerusalem who had assimilated into the Greek world. The historical and political circumstances at the time John was written, about 95 CE, and the significant theological differences and emphasis between John and the earlier three synoptic gospels writings accepted into the New Testament, supports the conclusion that John was written in response to the more formalized schism that came to exist between the majority of Jews who were not followers of Jesus, and those who were, along with the much larger group of Gentiles who were followers.

There is no intent to impugn the integrity or the sacredness of the faith and beliefs of the writer or writers of the beautifully written Gospel of John, or the Greek and Roman Gentiles who headed the Roman church during the first few centuries after Jesus' ministry. Nevertheless, the political and historical context of these times and their effects on present day Christianity should not be ignored. The Gospel of John provided the basis for the Roman and Greek Gentiles in the Church of Rome to diversify the oneness of God, and to move Christianity further away from the scriptures of Judaism. In the context of the still relevant pantheon of Greek and Roman gods and goddesses, and belief in a flat earth as the center of the universe, these would not have seemed such radical steps at the time.

The Deification of Jesus

Conflicting Scripture. Jesus says, *"The Father and I are one"* (John 10:30 and 17:11). God loved Jesus before the foundation of the world John (17:1-5, 24). Much more so than the other New Testament writings, John has the Jews that Jesus encounters believing that Jesus was claiming that he was equal to God (John 5:17-18). However, the Gospel of John creates an ambiguous message regarding Jesus' divinity, since Jesus also states, *"the Father is greater than I"* (John 14:28). The statements in John that Jesus and God are one create conflicts with Peter and Paul's letters. The statements in John also conflict with the three synoptic gospels; all of which depict Jesus as God's Son; particularly after Jesus' transfiguration. Regarding the transfiguration (2 Peter 1:16-21, Galatians 4:4-5, Acts 9:19-20, Matthew 17:1-13, Mark 9:2-8, Luke 9:28-36), Jesus took with him Peter, James and John:

> Suddenly a bright cloud overshadowed them, and from the cloud a voice said, "This is my Son, the Beloved; with him I am well pleased; listen to him!" (Matthew 17:5).

Paul states *"there is one God, the Father"* (1 Corinthians 8:6). Paul distinguishes Jesus from God. In Galatians 4:4-5, Paul states, *"God sent his Son, born of a woman, born under the law."* Paul, with his Jewish origins would most probably have strongly differed with John's characterization of Jesus and God as one, because the belief was blasphemous and heretical to the traditional Judaism concept of the unity of God. Similarly, the writers of the synoptic gospels, Mark, Matthew or Luke would most probably have differed with John's characterization of Jesus as God for the same reason.

The concept of the Jewish Messiah as God is contrary to ancient Judaic eschatology, which was that God had no equals. *"Hear O Israel: The Lord is our God. The Lord alone"* (Deuteronomy 6:4). Further, let the first of the Ten Commandments not be forgotten (Exodus 20:2-6) *"...you shall have no other gods before me...whether in the form of anything that is in heaven above or that is on the earth beneath, or that is in the water....You shall not bow down to them or worship them."*

Jesus' Riddle. Supporters of the "Jesus is God" theory point to Matthew 22:41-46; Mark 12:35-37; Luke 20:41-44, where Jesus asks the scribes and Pharisees, whose son is the Messiah, and the Pharisees respond that the Messiah is David's son. Jesus replies:

> How can the scribes say that the Messiah is the son of David? David himself, by the Holy Spirit declared, "The Lord said to my Lord, 'Sit at my right hand, until I put your enemies under your feet.'" David himself calls him Lord; so how can he be his son? (Mark 12:35-37).

Jesus' question was no doubt meant to confound the scribes and Pharisees in Matthew, the Sadducees in Mark and Luke, and perhaps everyone. Jesus is quoting from the first verse in David's Psalm 110, raising the question of whether the Messiah is merely a product of David's lineage, or something more. If the Messiah is more than a product of David's lineage, what is the Messiah in relation to God? Psalm 110 is set forth below:

> (1)The Lord says to my Lord, "Sit at my right hand until I make your enemies your footstool." (2) The Lord sends out from Zion your mighty scepter. Rule in the midst of your foes. (3) Your people will offer themselves willingly on the day you lead your forces on the holy mountains, like dew, your youth will come to you. (4) The Lord has sworn and will not change his mind, "You are a priest forever according to the order of Melchizedek." (5) The Lord is at your right hand; he will shatter kings on the day of his wrath. (6) He will execute judgment among the nations, filling them with corpses; he will shatter heads over the wide earth. (7) He will drink from the stream by the path; therefore he will lift up his head.

When read in its entirety Psalm 110 depicts the second Lord as a warrior-king who sits at the right hand of the first Lord, God, until the second Lord's enemies become his footstools. The second Lord will shatter kings, execute judgment among nations filling them with corpses, and shatter heads over the wide earth. This language doesn't describe Jesus very well. The reference could be to King Solomon, or perhaps even to Moshe Dayan, the Israeli general during the 1967 war between Israel, and Egypt, Syria and Jordan.

Unlike many of the Psalms which are essentially laments by David in the first person, Psalm 110 is a narration of a discussion, perhaps by David, between God and a second Lord. Significantly, in Psalm 110:4 the First Lord says to the second Lord, *"You are priest forever according to the order of Melchizedek."* The first biblical reference to the order of Melchizedek is in Genesis 14:18-20, where after Abram's defeat of Chedorlaomer and the kings who were with him, *"King Melchizedek of Salem brought out bread and wine; he was the priest of God Most High. He blessed Abram, and said, 'Blessed be Abram by God Most High ...'"*

King Melchizedek is mentioned in Hebrews 5:1-11, where Jesus is likened to being a priest forever according to the order of Melchizedek. Moreover, in Hebrews 7:11-17, we learn that:

> If perfection had been attainable through the Levitical priest-hood—for the people received the law under this priesthood—what further need were there have been to speak of another priest arising according to the order of Melchizedek, rather than according to the order of Aaron?…It is even more obvious when another priest arises, resembling Melchizedek, one who has become a priest, not through physical requirement concerning physical descent, but through the power of an indestructible life. For it is attested of him, "You are a priest according to the order of Melchizedek."

Hebrews indicates that God can select worthy mortals to become priests according to the order of Melchizedek. Jesus' riddle can be solved by imposing a priest according to the order of Melchizedek as the entity that David considered to be his Lord in Psalm 110. Psalm 110 provides no cogent evidence that Jesus is God.

Nicene Christianity. The differences in thinking between the early Christians and the later faction of Nicene Creed Christians, essentially, the Greek and Roman Gentiles in control of the church in Rome, can be seen in The Old Roman Symbol, which is an earlier and shorter version of the Apostles' Creed. During the second century certain Gnostic followers of Jesus believed that He was a divine being, lacking any human component. The Old Roman Symbol was developed as an affirmation of faith to ward off Gnostic believers by Jesus' followers who believed he was both spiritual and human. The following is an English translation of the Old Roman Symbol.

I believe in God the Father almighty;

and in Jesus Christ His only Son, our Lord,

Who was born from the Holy Spirit and the Virgin Mary,

Who under Pontius Pilate was crucified and buried,

on the third day rose again from the dead,

ascended into heaven,

sits at the right hand of the Father,

whence He will come to judge the living and the dead;

and in the Holy Spirit,

the holy Church,

the remission of sins,

the resurrection of the flesh,

(the life everlasting).

New Christians are to be baptized in the name of the Father, Son and Holy Spirit (Matthew 28:19). Blasphemy against the Holy Spirit will not be forgiven (Matthew 12:31-32). The Old Roman Symbol indicates that the Father, Son and Holy Spirit are separate entities. It makes no effort to equate the three and there is no allusion about the divinity of Jesus, or the Holy Spirit, and certainly no indication there would eventually be a Holy Trinity. The Holy Trinity does not reflect the original Christian understanding of the nature of Jesus as expressed by the three synoptic gospels or Mark, Matthew, Luke, Paul's letter, the Apostle's Creed and its predecessor, the Old Roman Symbol.

What was said in the PREFACE on these issues, though applicable, will not for the most part be repeated here. The Trinitarian concept was developed over a period of time to counter the beliefs of Macedonians, certain Gnostics and the followers of Arius of Alexandria whose beliefs varied from one another, but were alike in that none believed that Jesus or the Holy Spirit was God. Under the theory of the Holy Trinity, the Father, Son and Holy Spirit all comprise God. Each of these separate and divine entities is at the same time fully God. Each of these entities is also fully distinct. Each of these entities has unique functions. Though they function separately, they are united in purpose and function as one God.

Arius of Alexandria was an influential and scholarly priest. He was aware of the conflict created by the Gospel of John and the earlier writings. He was familiar with Origen of Alexandria's (185-254) writings, Origen's similar understanding of God and Jesus, and the views of Gnostic Christians. In the 4th century, to counter the developing belief that Jesus and God were equals, as promoted by portions of the gospel of John, Arius refined the Origen concept of Jesus. Arius concluded that the Father alone was God. A belief in the full deity of Jesus would mean that there were two separate Gods. Arius concluded that Jesus was not born eternal or divine by nature. Jesus' nature became divine through his obedience to God. Thus, humans, can be born again through the example of Jesus Christ, and be resurrected and given eternal life by God.

Arius was opposed in his beliefs by the Bishop of Alexandria, Athanasius. Athanasius served as the Bishop of Alexandria over a span of 47 years, though he spent 17 years of those years in various exiles as a consequence of the orders of various Roman Emperors. As a consequence of the Gospel of John the issue of Jesus' divinity was debated until 325 CE, when the Council of Nicaea was convened. The council was convened at the urging of the Roman Emperor, Constantine I, the first emperor to convert to Christianity and make Christianity the official religion of the Roman Empire. The controversy was virulent at the time. Resolving it would help Constantine's ability to rule his subjects. Constantine presided over the Council, and it was clear at the time that many of the church leaders were awed and somewhat intimidated by the emperor's presence as the host of the gathering.

Many but not all prominent theologians attended the Council. These theologians were compelled to come to a definitive decision and feared failing Constantine. At the time, though Constantine had allegedly converted to Christianity, he had not been baptized as a Christian. He did not want to be baptized until he was on his death bed. He feared if he were baptized too early, he would sin again and not attain salvation and the kingdom of heaven. Ultimately, church clergy attending the Council concluded that Jesus was God and not the Son of God. The Eastern Church that would be based in Constantinople continued in its Arian beliefs.

Eventually, Roman Emperor Theodosius I convened the First Council of Constantinople in 381 CE that confirmed the Nicene beliefs and added the Holy Spirit to the concept of God. Its conclusions were not confirmed as ecumenical until 451 CE at the Council of Chalcedon. Thus, largely due to the influence of Roman emperor governance and politics, the Holy Trinity officially became a church doctrine, though controversy remained. Even today there is an irreconcilable dispute between Roman Catholic and Eastern Orthodox Christians as to whether the Holy Spirit emanates from the Father and the Son, or only from the Father. This is the so called *filioque issue.*

The belief in the theory that the Holy Spirit, Jesus and God are one appears to be irrelevant as related to the concept of salvation. It has little to do with the self-sacrifice and the faith-based *actions-works* taught by Jesus. Equating Jesus with God also complicates the belief in the death and resurrection of Jesus. God is immortal. God cannot die and raise Himself. God cannot suffer. Jesus had doubts at Gethsemane before his betrayal, trial and crucifixion (Matthew 26:36-46, Mark 14:32-42). He cried out before he died on the cross, *"My God, my God, why have you forsaken me?"* (Matthew 27:46, Mark 15:34).

In addition to the deification of Jesus, the Nicene form of Christianity also raised the prominence of the Apostle Paul and diminished the prominence of Jesus in what became the official form of Nicene Christian beliefs. The Gentiles who became the followers of Jesus greatly outnumbered the Jewish followers of Jesus. The Gentiles were essentially the Romans and Greeks of that period. They formed the hierarchy of the early church structure and were in a position to form and influence its beliefs and dogma. The context of their world was the pantheon of multiple gods and goddesses and a flat earth which was the center of their universe. Their interests were in developing and distinguishing a body of beliefs and distinguishing those beliefs from Judaic beliefs.

As stated previously, a review of scripture indicates that Jesus was fearful and overcome at Gethsemane when confronted with facing his destiny. Jesus knew he was facing betrayal, trial, crucifixion and death. He asked God that if it were possible, to let the cup pass from him; but that it should not be what [Jesus] wanted, but what God wanted (Matthew 26:36-46, Luke 22:39-46). Jesus bowed to God's will and went through with his arrest, trial and crucifixion. Jesus offered prayers and supplications, with loud cries and tears to the one who was able to save him from his death, (Hebrews 5:7). He cried out on the cross asking why God had forsaken him, (Mark 15:34, Matthew 27:45-50).

Jesus conveyed God's message for how humanity must live to achieve the kingdom of heaven. In doing so Jesus was obedient to God to the end in demonstrating his faith and earning his status as God's Son by that demonstration. However, Gentiles, through Paul's message, became the primary followers of Jesus. The emphasis on Jesus' ministry was largely diminished. The beliefs of Pelagius, Arius, Origen and others were defeated and relegated to heresy.

Paul and John's theories emphasizing accepting and worshipping Jesus, rather than emphasizing the requirements of Jesus' ministry as in the synoptic gospels, became the predominant Nicene Christian dogma. Paul's profound faith in Jesus as the giver of eternal life for Gentiles and Jews was the motivator for Paul's own faith and his zealous efforts to convert Gentiles. However, Paul, as a Pharisee, already believed in a resurrection of the body. Paul's message of accepting Jesus as Lord and

Savior has little to do with Jesus' message of living and demonstrating obedience to God in accordance with Jesus' ministry. The degradation of present day Christianity and its affect on the degradation of our democracy, our confiscatory concentration of wealth, and the deprivation of the rights of the large majority are proof.

As stated above, there is no intent to impugn the integrity or the sacredness of the faith or good intentions of the writer or writers of the beautifully written Gospel of John, or the Gentiles who headed the Roman church during the first few centuries after Jesus' ministry. Nevertheless, the political and historical context of these times and their effects on present day Christianity should not be ignored. The Gospel of John provided the basis for the Roman and Greek Gentiles in the Church of Rome to dilute and diversify the oneness of God, and to move Christianity further away from the scriptures of Judaism. In the context of the still relevant pantheon of Greek and Roman gods and goddesses, and belief in a flat earth as the center of the universe, these would not have seemed such radical steps at the time.

Chapter 5.

THE REFORMATION: JUSTIFICATION BY FAITH: PREDESTINATION

The Reformation

Before the Nicene form of Christianity became the official church religion within the Roman Empire in the late 5th century, the church in Rome had already accelerated its activities of centralizing and imposing its practices, beliefs and dogma on the widespread churches within the Roman Empire. The centralization involved not only the imposition of practices, beliefs and dogma on other churches, but the stamping out of what the church considered to be errant beliefs, practices and dogma. Some examples of these impositions included belief in the Holy Trinity, recitation of the Nicene Creed and the establishment of the original sin theory as fundamental Christian beliefs. The church abolished widespread Gnostic beliefs and writings among other Christians.

During the Middle Ages the church in Rome, which had established its supremacy and control throughout western Europe, had been enriching itself from the sale of indulgences by its clergy; a practice that allowed the nobility and the wealthy to allegedly receive the forgiveness of their sins by the church for the payment of money, the transfer of land, or for political favors. Through the early 16th century, the prevailing Roman Catholic theory for the salvation of believers was that works were needed to perfect faith, and that without works, faith was dead. The indulgences were considered a form of works.

Raised and educated during the time of indulgences, Martin Luther (1483-1546), a prominent church theologian who considered the indulgences to be repugnant, concluded, like Paul, that God's alleged act of declaring a sinner righteous by faith in Jesus alone was sufficient for salvation. There was no need for anything additional such as works, which he considered indulgences to be. In Martin Luther's case, rather than concluding that the buying or selling of indulgences was an aberrant practice and not works, he proceeded to abolish the need for any types of works to perfect faith. He concluded that justification is a gift from God that humans cannot achieve through any works of their own. He appears to have treated justification by faith alone as equivalent to salvation.

Martin Luther placed the biblical books of Hebrews, James, Jude and Revelation at the end of his version of the New Testament on the basis that they lacked the stature of the other books. There is evidence that Luther sought to have the Letter of James removed from the Bible. Scholars debate Luther's motives, especially regarding the letter of James, which directly contradicts Luther's assertion that faith alone is sufficient for salvation without the need for faith-based works. It is difficult to see how Martin Luther might have rationalized Jesus' statement that "not everyone who says to me 'Lord, Lord' will enter the kingdom of heaven, but only the one who does the will of my father in heaven" (Matthew 7:21-23). Doing the will of the Father in heaven involves faith-works; not faith alone as Martin Luther contends.

Martin Luther did not intend to form a separate church or churches. However, he challenged Papal authority regarding church teachings and beliefs, concluding that reliance on his interpretation of the Bible was the only source for divinely revealed knowledge. He was ex-communicated from the church. His beliefs and his ex-communication ultimately resulted in the founding of Lutheranism. A generation later, John Calvin (1509-1564), another prominent theologian agreed with Martin Luther and furthered what became the Protestant Reformation in other parts of Europe.

The Eastern Orthodox Church had always remained distinct in its practices and beliefs from the Roman Catholic Church and never acquired the sale of indulgence practices. Consequently, the Orthodoxy was not affected by the Reformation and continued in the centuries' old tradition and belief that faith-based works were needed to perfect faith, and that faith without these works was not enough to achieve salvation. Justification in the Orthodox Church does not play a significant role. In the words of one church bishop:

> Justification is not a once-for-all, instantaneous pronouncement guaranteeing eternal salvation. Justification is a living, dynamic, day-to-day reality for the one who follows Christ. The Christian actively pursues a righteous life in the grace and power of God granted to all who believe in Him.

The Roman Catholic Church convened the Council of Trent between the years 1545 and 1563 where it sought to counter the Reformation movement and reevaluate the practices that had been considered objectionable. Though the sale of indulgences, as such, was abolished, the centuries old belief that faith-based works to perfect faith were needed for salvation remained the doctrine of the Church. The Eastern Orthodox church's dogma that faith based works were a demonstration of faith and essential for salvation has never wavered. Most Protestant churches follow Martin Luther and John Calvin's beliefs.

Justification by Faith Alone

There is no definition of justification, justification by faith alone, or salvation in the Bible. Thus, the meanings must be derived by focusing on how the words are used in scripture; not an easy task because of the inconsistent use of the words. Focusing first on justification, Paul uses the word "justified" in Romans 3:4, where he quotes scripture stating, "*So that you might be justified in your words, and prevail in your judging.*" Paul is referring to Psalm 51:4 which provides, "*so that you are justified in your sentence and blameless when you pass judgment.*" Paul's use of the word "justified" is consistent with its present day, non-religious usage. As used, the word *justified* means that whoever is imposing a sentence, or judging, has done so with merit, or for sound reasons.

In Romans 3:20 Paul states, "*no human being will be justified in his sight by deeds prescribed by the law, for through the law comes the knowledge of sin.*" Here, Paul is citing Psalm 143:2, "*for no one living is righteous before you.*" Thus, within Romans, Paul first uses the word justified to mean having sound reason and merit, and then to state that no one is righteous, that is, living without sin. In Romans 3:23-24, Paul states, "*since all have sinned...they are now justified [made righteous] by his grace...*" In Roman 4:25 Paul states, "*[Jesus], who was handed over to death for our trespasses and was raised for our justification [righteousness].*" In Romans 5:1, Paul states that, "*Therefore, since we are justified [made righteous] by faith, we have peace with God through our Lord Jesus Christ.*" And in Romans 5:16, Paul states that, "*the free gift following many trespasses brings justification [righteousness].*"

Though Paul uses the word *justified* to mean righteous or righteousness, the meaning of righteous or righteousness remains unclear. Thus, justification by faith alone, or righteousness by faith alone does not translate directly to salvation. Accordingly, based on the use of the words in the scriptures, it is unclear what justification by faith alone means, or what Martin Luther meant by his use of that term.

For most Protestants, justification is a singular act, relying on 2 Corinthians 5:21, *"For our sake he [God] made him [Jesus] to be sin who knew no sin, so that in him we might become the righteousness of God." "For we hold that a person is justified by faith apart from works prescribed by the law"* (Romans 3:28). Paul is stating that faith in Jesus is required for justification, and that justification cannot be achieved through works prescribed by law. However, the context for Paul's statement was Paul's lesson for Jews who were not followers of Jesus. It was also Paul's lesson for Gentiles that it was not necessary to become Jews to achieve justification. Paul's Galatians 2:16 and 3:5-6, are essentially a repeat of Romans 3:28. Paul appears to be talking here about justification [righteousness], not about salvation.

Regarding salvation, "Lead me in your truth and teach me for you are the God of my salvation" (Psalm 25:5), and *"Let us make a joyful noise to the rock of our salvation"* (Psalm 95:1). The use of the word "salvation" in the Old Testament is interesting, because the Sadducees, who maintained the Temple and controlled the sacrificial practices, did not believe in a resurrection and an afterlife. The Pharisees, who studied the law, believed in a resurrection and an afterlife. Salvation is frequently referred to in the Psalms which predated the Sadducees and the Pharisees.

In Romans 5:8-9, Paul states, *"God proves his love for us, for while we were still sinners Christ died for us. Much more surely then, now that we have been justified by his blood, we will be saved through him from the wrath of God."* Paul states *"we will be saved,"* after being justified. Again, though it is not entirely clear what Paul means by justification, justification can lead to salvation, but to be justified is not itself salvation, or being saved.

In 1 Corinthians 1:8, 3:12-15, 2 Corinthians 2:15 and Philippians 2:12 Paul states that believers will be saved. Continuing to focus on salvation, *"And all the flesh shall see the salvation of God"* (Luke 3:6), quoting Isaiah. *"Salvation belongs to our God who is seated on the throne and to the Lamb"* (Revelations 7:10). In all these passages salvation is a future event, not a living, or present event as in justification.

John 3:16 provides that, *"For God so loved the world that he gave his only begotten Son, that everyone who believes in Him may not perish but have eternal life."* This statement in John can be interpreted so that salvation already exists for the believer. However, in faith, as in the law, this statement can best be defined as dictum. Dictum is a judicial statement or opinion on a point, other than the precise issue involved in deciding the outcome of the particular case. John may not be outlining the entire process needed for salvation, but only one element; belief in Jesus. In this case, salvation; *"anyone who believes in Him may not perish but have eternal life,"* could also depend on how that belief in Jesus moves the believer to accomplish what Jesus preached. The question can also be asked that if *"God so loved the world"* why was it inflicted with original sin?

Contrary to Paul's verses above inferring that salvation is a future event, in Romans 8:24, Paul states, *"For in hope we were saved."* See also Ephesians 2:8 where Paul states *"For by grace you have been saved through faith, and this is not your doing it is the gift of God."* Here, Paul is preaching that salvation cannot be earned, speaks of believers as having been saved, rather than being saved sometime in the future.

On the question of what is needed for salvation; Jesus was moved by the contributions of the poor widow who had little, over the wealthy who contributed from their abundance (Mark 12:41-44). Jesus was impressed because of the widow's giving based on her self-sacrifice. James says faith by itself without works is dead (James 3:14-17). Even Paul says, *"... work out your own salvation with fear and trembling"* (Philippians 2:12-14).

James says:

> Show me your faith apart from your works, and I by my works
> will show you my faith… Was not our ancestor Abraham justi-
> fied by works when he offered his son, Isaac on the alter? You
> see that faith was active along with his works….Thus the scrip-
> ture was fulfilled that says, "Abraham believed God, and it was
> reckoned to him as righteousness," and he was called the friend
> of God. You see that a person is justified by works and not by
> faith alone (James 2:18-24).

Regarding salvation being based on more than just faith in Jesus,
Jesus says, *"Enter through the narrow gate for the gate is wide and the
road is easy that leads to destruction, and there are many who take it.
For the gate is narrow and the road is hard that leads to life, and there
are few who find it"* (Matthew 7:13-14). *"Not everyone who says to me
'Lord, Lord' will enter the kingdom of heaven, but only the one who
does the will of my Father in heaven. On that day many will say to me
'Lord, Lord, did we not prophesy in your name, and cast out demons
in your name, and do many deeds of power in your name?' Then I will
declare to them, 'I never knew you; go away from me, you evildoer'"*
(Matthew 7:21-23).

Predestination

One of the concepts undergirding Christianity is the concept of free
will. Salvation is theoretically available to any person, depending on
whether that person exercises their free will in a manner pleasing to
God, or whether a believer accepts Jesus as their Lord and Savior, as
believers in justification by faith alone contend. Nevertheless, several
early prominent Christians, including the Apostle Paul, believed in predestination, which conflicts not only with the concept of free will, but
also with a life of faith-based works, or accepting Jesus as the path to
salvation.

The Bing Dictionary reference definition of predestination is *"the divine foreordination of all that will happen, especially with regard to the salvation of some, but not of others."* The Wikipedia definition of predestination is *"a doctrine or theory that all events have been willed by God, usually with reference to the eventual fate of the individual soul."* Though the subject of predestination is often ignored in Christianity's teachings because of the inherent conflict with fundamental Christian concepts, there are strong elements of predestination in scripture and in official Christian pronouncements.

Friedrich Nietzsche, the 19th century philosopher, was a critic of Judeo-Christian morality and a believer in the philosophy of Determinism. One element of Determinism is the belief that humans are incapable of controlling future events, and incapable of controlling their destiny. An implication of determinism is that humans have no free will, and thus, cannot be held responsible for their actions. Predestination is the antithesis of Christianity, because predestination will relegate at least some persons to salvation, or no salvation, irrespective of their faith in Jesus or their faith-based good works.

To begin with, God in the Old Testament chose Abel over Cain (Genesis 4:2-5). God also chose Jacob over elder son Esau to receive God's blessing (Genesis 28:10-15), even though Jacob used deceit and artifice to convince his blind and senile father, Isaac, to bless Jacob rather than Esau with the family inheritance and leadership responsibilities (Genesis 27:18-29). There apparently was no amount of faith or faith-based works that Esau could do to change God's disdain, and no amount of deceit and artifice that Jacob could perpetrate to change God's love.

As another example, it is difficult to see how *"all the families of the earth shall be blessed"* if you were a Canaanite in the town of Ai, where men and women, were slaughtered, their livestock taken, and the town burned, to satisfy God's promise (Joshua 8:24-30). The ancient Hebrews occupied land on which they had not labored, towns they had not built, and ate and harvested food they had not worked for (Joshua 24:13). God's killing the first born of the Pharaohs is another example of God's inscrutability (Exodus 12:29-32).

In considering the destruction of Sodom and Gomorrah, God agreed that he would not destroy the towns if there were ten righteous persons there (Genesis 18:24-33). Ultimately, the towns were destroyed except for Lott and his two daughters (Genesis 19:30). Though Lot's wife was initially saved, she was destroyed when she looked back (Genesis 19:24).

Turning to the New Testament, Revelations 7:4 and 14:1-5 provide that 144,000 persons from the 12 tribes of Israel will be marked with a seal on their foreheads prior to the destruction. *"It is these who have not been defiled themselves with women, for they are virgins; these follow the lamb wherever he goes. They have been redeemed from humankind as the first fruits for God and the Lamb, and in their mouth no lie has been found; they are blameless."*

Paul's statements in Romans 9:11-16 indicate that Paul held views consistent with predestination, and with certain elements of determinism, notwithstanding Paul's views that anyone and everyone could achieve salvation through belief in Jesus. Referring to God speaking to Rebecca regarding the offspring of Isaac and Rebecca, Paul stated:

> Even before they had been born or done anything good or bad (so that God's purpose of election might continue, not by works but by his call) she was told,
>
> > The elder shall serve the younger. As it is written, I have loved Jacob, but have hated Esau.
>
> What then are we to say? Is there injustice on God's part? By no means! For [God] says to Moses,

> I shall show mercy on whom I have mercy, and I will
> have compassion on whom I have compassion.

So it depends not on human will or exertion, but on God who shows mercy. Paul's views on Predestination are also supported by Romans 8:28-30, where Paul states:

> We know that all things work together for good for those who love God who are called according to his purpose. For those whom he foreknew he also predestined to be conformed to the image of his own Son, in order that he be the first born within a large family. And those whom he predestined he also called; and those whom he called he also justified; and those whom he justified he also glorified.

Paul appears to distinguish between predestination that was applicable to the ancient Israelites based on their striving for righteousness based on works, from the faith-based righteousness available through Jesus Christ for Gentiles and for Jews who accept Jesus. In Romans 9:30-33 Paul states:

> What then are we to say? Gentiles, who did not strive for righteousness, have attained it, that is, righteousness through faith; but Israel who did strive for righteousness that is based on the law, did not succeed in fulfilling the law. Why not? Because they did not strive for it on the basis of faith, but as if it were based on works. They have stumbled …

Contrary to these statements in Romans, Paul also states God desires everyone to be saved.

> First of all, then, I urge that supplications, prayers, intercessions, and thanksgivings be made for everyone, for kings and all who are in high positions, so that we may lead a quiet and peaceable life in all godliness and dignity. This is right and acceptable in

the sight of God our Savior, who desires everyone to be saved and to come to the knowledge of the truth (1 Timothy 2:1-4).

Taken as a whole, Paul's writings regarding predestination are ambiguous. Contrary to predestination beliefs of Paul, Peter states:

The Lord is not slow about his promise, as some may think of slowness, but is patient with you, not wanting any person to perish, but all to come to repentance (2 Peter 3:9).

The concept of predestination can be found in the writings of St. Augustine (354–430), St. Thomas Aquinas (1225–1274) and John Calvin (1509–1564). Two issues raised by predestination involve the fairness of God and the power of free will. Consistent with Paul's statements in Romans, St. Augustine believed that the reasons for God's choices are inscrutable. St. Augustine's reasoning is that God's choice to bless Jacob and not Esau might be inequitable in human terms, but not unjust, because neither Jacob not Esau deserved God's blessing, but that God bestowed his blessing on Esau because God is merciful.

While there is considerable equivocation and ambiguity in present day Christian views that all can be saved, if God is God, it appears that God has reserved the right to make inscrutable choices as he did with Cain and Abel, and with Jacob and Esau.

Chapter 6.

WHAT WERE JESUS' TEACHINGS?

Jesus placed no emphasis on his followers worshipping Him. Jesus placed little or no importance on his followers believing in his nature. He placed no importance on his followers believing he was equal to God. He placed no importance on believing in the Holy Trinity. He placed no importance on believing in the concept of original sin. Jesus did not preach that justification by faith alone, without faith-based works, was sufficient for salvation. Jesus was selfless. God didn't send Jesus to be worshipped. God sent Jesus to teach humanity to live in accordance with God's requirements.

The gospels relate that Jesus performed many miracles including healing the sick, the blind, the infirm, calming the storm, walking on water, and multiplying the fish and bread. Resisting evil and performing the miracles and healings demonstrated Jesus' nature, the power of faith, love, and obedience to God. They are not included here with Jesus' teachings. Similarly, Jesus' travels, betrayal, crucifixion and resurrection are not included. Jesus' ministry and teachings that follow are focused on Jesus' messages for doing the Father's will in heaven. Jesus is best described as a selfless purveyor of God's message for humanity.

To begin with, Jesus taught us to resist the evil temptations of grandeur, power and riches that he was tempted with in the wilderness by the devil. After fasting for 40 days, being famished, and then being tempted to turn stones into loaves of bread, Jesus replied: *"One does not live by bread alone, but by every word that comes out of the mouth of God."* When he was taken to the pinnacle of the temple, and tempted to throw himself down because he would be saved, Jesus replied: *"Do not put the Lord your God to the test."* Again, when tempted with receiving all the kingdoms of the world and their splendor, Jesus replied: *"Worship the Lord your God, and serve only him"* (Matthew 4:1-11, Luke 4:1-13). Resisting temptations is a lifelong quest, not dealt with very easily, and not always successfully.

To begin His ministry Jesus stated that:

> The Spirit of the Lord is upon me, because he has anointed me to bring good news to the poor. He has sent me to proclaim release to the captives and recovery of sight to the blind, to let the oppressed go free, to proclaim the year of the Lord's favor (Luke 4:18-19).

> Blessed are the poor in spirit, for theirs is the kingdom of heaven.
> Blessed are those who mourn, for they will be comforted.
> Blessed are the meek, for they will inherit the earth.
> Blessed are those who hunger and thirst for righteousness, for they will be filled.
> Blessed are the merciful, for they will receive mercy.
> Blessed are the pure of heart, for they will see God.
> Blessed are the peacemakers, for they will be called children of God.

Blessed are those who are persecuted for righteousness sake, for theirs is the kingdom of heaven.

Blessed are you when people…persecute you…on my account…for your reward is great in heaven…(Matthew 5:3-12).

Blessed are you who are poor, for yours is the kingdom of God. Blessed are you who are hungry now, for you will be filled. Blessed are you who weep now, for you will laugh. Blessed are you when people…defame you on account of the Son of Man… for surely your reward is great in heaven (Luke 6:20-23.

…Come you that are blessed by my Father, inherit the kingdom prepared for you from the foundation of the world; for I was hungry and you gave me food, I was thirsty and you gave me something to drink, I was a stranger and you welcomed me, I was naked and you gave me clothing, I was sick and you took care of me, I was in prison and you visited me.…Then the righteous will answer him, "Lord, when was it that we saw you Hungry and gave you food, or thirsty and gave you something to drink? And when was it we saw you a stranger and welcomed you, or naked and gave you clothing? And when was it that we saw you sick or in prison and visited you"? And the king will answer them, "Truly, I tell you, just as you did it to one of the least of these who are members of my family, you did it to me" (Matthew 25: 34-40).

Jesus, speaking to his disciples said: *"If any want to become my followers, let them deny themselves and take up their crosses and follow me"* (Matthew 16:24, Mark 8:34, Luke 9:23). Give and assist not just from your abundance but with love and self-sacrifice. This is seldom mentioned or preached in today's churches. Jesus was not impressed with the large sums, contributed by the wealthy, but from those whose giving came at the expense of self-deprivation. Indeed, Jesus' entire life was one of self-sacrifice and deprivation in conveying God's message and in the furtherance of God's purposes.

[Jesus] sat down opposite the treasury, and watched the crowd putting money into the treasury. Many rich people put in large sums. A poor widow came and put in two small copper coins, which are worth a penny. Then he called the disciples and said to them, "Truly I tell you, this poor widow has put in more than all those who are contributing to the treasury. For all of them have contributed out of their abundance; but she out of her poverty has put in everything she had, all she had to live on" (Mark 12:41-44, Luke 21:1-4).

Despite the message predominating in many of today's churches, Christianity is not "a feel good" religion. Before his death on the cross Jesus cried out, *"My God, My God, Why have you forsaken me?"* (Mark 15:34, Matthew 27:46). These words are the opening words of David's lengthy Psalm 22, part of which is quoted below:

My God, my God, why have you forsaken me? Why are you so far from helping me, from the words of my groaning? O my God, I cry by day, but you do not answer; and by night, but find no rest. Yet you are holy, enthroned on the praises of Israel. In you our ancestors trusted; they trusted and you delivered them. To you they cried, and were saved; in you they trusted, and were not put to shame... But you O Lord, do not be far away! O my help, come quickly to my aid!... To him, indeed, shall all who sleep in the earth bow down; before him shall bow down all who go down to the dust, and I shall live for him. Posterity will serve him; future generations will be told about the Lord, and proclaim his deliverance to a people yet unborn, saying that he has done it (Psalms 22:1-5, 19, 29-31).

Jesus' lament while dying on the cross was expressed in the writings of Mother Teresa, as reported in *Time* by David Van Biema in reviewing the book entitled, *Mother Teresa: Come Be My Light*, written by the Rev. Brian Kolodiejchuk. Mother Teresa spent her life ministering to the needs of the poor, the hungry, the sick, the elderly and the dying on the streets of India. In her public statements Mother Teresa said, *"It is not enough for us to say I love God, but I do not love my neighbor… Jesus' hunger is what you and I must find and alleviate."*

Regarding salvation being based on more than just faith in Jesus, Jesus says, *"In everything do to others as you would have them do to you; for this is the law and the prophets"* (Matthew 7:12). *"Enter through the narrow gate; for the gate is wide and the road is easy that leads to destruction, and there are many who take it. For the gate is narrow and the road is hard that leads to life, and there are few who find it"* (Matthew 7:13-14).… *"Not everyone who says to me 'Lord, Lord' will enter the kingdom of heaven, but only the one who does the will of my Father in heaven. On that day many will say to me 'Lord, Lord did we not prophesy in your name, and cast out demons in your name, and do many deeds of power in your name?' Then I will declare to them, 'I never knew you, go away from me you evildoers'"* (Matthew 7:21-23).

Quoted below is Jesus' general advice and admonishment relating to the difficulty of entering the kingdom of heaven. There is little sympathy for the rich for they already have their consolation, as Jesus' quotes indicate. When a rich man who had followed the commandments his whole life asked Jesus how he could inherit the kingdom of heaven, Jesus advised him to sell all his goods and give the money to the poor, and he would have treasure in heaven (Matthew 19:16-22, Mark 10:17-22, Luke 18:18-25).

Truly I tell you, it will be hard for a rich man to enter the kingdom of heaven. Again I tell you, it is easier for a camel to go through the eye of a needle than for someone who is rich to enter the kingdom of God....And everyone who has left houses or brothers and sisters or father or mother or children or fields, for my name's sake, will receive a hundredfold, and will inherit eternal life. But many who are first will be last, and the last will be first (Matthew 19:23-30, Mark 10:23-25, Luke 14:25-27, Luke 18:24-30).

But woe to you who are rich, for you have received your consolation. Woe to you who are full now, for you will be hungry. Woe to you who are laughing now, for you will mourn and weep. Woe to you when all speak well of you, for that is what their ancestors did to the false prophets (Luke 6:24-26).

Do not store up for yourselves treasures on earth....You cannot serve God and wealth (Matthew 6:19-24, Luke 12:16-21).

Beware of false profits, who come to you in sheep's clothing, but inwardly are ravenous wolves (Matthew 7:13-15, Luke 13:23-29).

Jesus' ministry occurred during the reign of the Roman Empire and the subjugation of the ancient Israelites. Jesus' teachings included the need for direct participation in justice and challenging the existing order. Again, these are seldom mentioned or preached in today's churches.

Do not think I have come to bring peace to the earth; I have not come to bring peace, but a sword. I have come to set man against father, daughter against mother,...Whoever loves father and mother more than me...and whoever does not take up the cross and follow me is not worthy of me. Those who find their life will lose it, and those who lose their life for my sake will find it (Matthew 10:34-39). My mother and my brothers are those who hear the word of God and do it (Luke 8:21).

I came to bring fire to the earth, and how I wish it were already kindled!... Do you think I have come to bring peace to the earth? No, I tell you, but rather division! ... father against son, mother against daughter, and daughter against mother, mother-in-law against daughter-in-law and daughter-in-law against mother-in-law (Luke 12:49-53).

If any want to become my followers, let them deny themselves and take up their cross and follow me. For those that want to save their life will lose it, and those who lose their life for my sake will find it. For what will it profit them if they gain the whole world but forfeit their life? Or what will they give in return for their life? (Matthew 16:24-26, Mark 8:34-38, Luke 9:23-25)

Jesus' views on the commandments are set forth below.

You shall love the Lord your God with all your heart, and with all your soul, and with all your mind. This is the greatest and first commandment. And a second is like it: You shall love your neighbor as yourself. On these two commandments hang all the law and the prophets. This is much more important than all whole burnt offerings and sacrifices (Matthew 5:17-20, 22:37-40, Mark 12:28-31, 12:30-33).

In everything do to others as you would have them do to you (Matthew 7:12, Luke 6:31).

You shall have no other gods before me. You shall not make for yourself an idol ...

You shall not make wrongful use of the name of the Lord your God ...

Remember the Sabbath day, and keep it holy...

Honor your mother and your father...

> You shall not commit murder.
>
> You shall not commit adultery.
>
> You shall not steal.
>
> You shall not covet your neighbor's house…wife, or…anything that belongs to your neighbor…
>
> (Exodus 20:1-17, Deuteronomy 5:6-21).

> You have heard that it was said to those of ancient times, "You shall not commit murder," and "whoever murders shall be liable to judgment." But I say to you that if you are angry with a brother or sister you will be liable to judgment.…So when you are offering your gift at the altar, if you remember your brother or sister has something against you, leave your gift there before the alter and go; first be reconciled to your brother or sister, and then come and offer your gift (Matthew 5:21-24).

The admonishment against anger is consistent with the Lord's Prayer which requires the forgiveness of debts or trespasses in exchange for God's forgiveness of debts or trespasses. A reasonable interpretation requires an engagement for this purpose to be a good-faith attempt at reconciliation. Perhaps some brothers or sisters may not be reconcilable. Jesus himself became angry at the money changers in the temple (Matthew 21:12, Mark 11:15-16). Jesus' anger resulted because the money changers, scribes' and Pharisees' were desecrating God's temple with their activities.

In today's society where visual objectification is paramount for the unsavory purposes of the promotion of materialism and over-consumption, Jesus' admonishments provide an awakening.

> You have heard that it was said, "You shall not commit adultery". But I say to you that everyone who looks at a woman with lust has already committed adultery with her in his heart (Matthew 5:27-28).

"Lust" is defined in Webster's Dictionary as having an intense desire or sexual urge. Hopefully, this is what Jesus had in mind. Perhaps lust can then be distinguished from the appreciation of creation or beauty. Appreciating or admiring the Grand Canyon, the scenic Yosemite National park, a painting, a ballet, or a beautiful man or woman is hopefully, not lust. Equating lust with adultery appears to be equating objectionable thoughts with objectionable behavior. It would appear that lusting and not committing adultery is less objectionable and ultimately less hurtful than the actual commission of adultery, but that's not what scripture says.

On the subject of divorce, Jesus stated:

> It was also said, "Whoever divorces his wife, let him give her a certificate of divorce. But I say to you anyone who divorces his wife, except on grounds of unchastity, causes her to commit adultery; and whoever marries a divorced woman commits adultery" (Matthew 5:31-32).

The Pharisees, intending to impugn Jesus' statement about divorce, stated that Moses allowed a man to write a certificate of dismissal to divorce a wife. Jesus stated that it was only because they had hardened their hearts that Moses wrote the commandment for them, stating further that *"what God has joined together, let no one separate"* (Matthew 19:3-6). *"Whoever divorces his wife and marries another commits adultery against her; and if she divorces her husband and marries another, she commits adultery"* (Mark 10:2-12).

Regarding the subject of divorce and other matters, many church Fathers and Christian theologians interpreted the Bible allegorically, as having hidden spiritual meaning transcending the literal word. Today we have the biblical literalist. Many biblical literalists strongly believe that no one has the authority or right to reinterpret Jesus' clear proscription against divorce, or about any other matter about which Jesus has spoken. However, biblical literalists must remember that it was Jesus who saved the adulterous woman from being stoned, asserting to her accusers that the one without sin should cast the first stone (John 8:1-11).

In terms of imposing biblical context, the Bible allows the enslavement of aliens and the taking of slaves from other nations (Leviticus 25:44-45). A daughter could be sold into slavery. The offspring of slaves became slaves (Exodus 21:2-7). Slaves were required to accept the beating of their masters (1 Peter 2:18-21). Jesus' parables depict cruel treatment of slaves who suffer violence, beatings and death, all without condemnation by Jesus (Matthew 18:23-35, 21:33-44, Mark 12:1-12, Luke 19:11-17, 20:9-18). Hopefully, biblical literalists would not return us to the inhumanity of slavery, the subjugation of Native-Americans, or to women's inability to own property or vote.

While there is no intention here of minimizing the proscriptions against and the effects of divorce, some context might be helpful. In biblical times women were essentially considered chattel, personal property, with no means of independently supporting themselves except through marriage. Thus, a woman would generally be forced to turn to prostitution if she were divorced. The biblical proscription against divorce can be viewed as intended to protect women at the time. However, in today's world women are entitled to vote, inherit and own property. There are laws prohibiting discrimination in the workplace; laws requiring equal pay; and the establishment of alimony and child support in the event of a divorce or separation. Thus, it can be argued that in today's world the proscription against divorce is no longer needed.

Jesus advised turning the other cheek when struck (Matthew 5:39, Luke 6:29). While turning the other cheek might be appropriate in certain circumstance, today the striking of a cheek by another is generally the criminal act of assault and battery, punishable by imprisonment or at least with fines for minor offenses.

You have heard that it was said, "An eye for an eye and a tooth for a tooth." But I say to you. Do not resist an evildoer. But if anyone strikes you on the right cheek, turn the other also... Give to everyone who begs from you, and do not refuse anyone who wants to borrow from you" (Matthew 5:38-42, Luke 6:30).

This is an example of practicing the Christian faith by being magnanimous. Not refusing anyone who wants to borrow from you, might depend on the history of the relationship, if any, the immediacy of the need, the likelihood that the assistance will make a difference, and the ability of the giver to satisfy the request, given other obligations. When a borrower asks for money for food for herself and her child, but refuses an offer to pay for their meals at a nearby restaurant, there is some assurance that the request for the money was for a need other than for food.

Jesus became angry with the scribes and Pharisees who refused to answer whether it was proper for Jesus to cure a man with a withered hand on the Sabbath (Mark 3:1-6, Matthew 23:23-24, Luke 6:41-42). The scribes and Pharisees were concerning themselves more with the letter of the law as a means to empower themselves over the people, rather than concerning themselves with the spirit of the law to serve the people.

Administering to those who love you has little relevance in terms of value towards salvation, for even the tax collectors and sinners love those who love them. It seems that deeds worthy of salvation need to be done for truly charitable and altruistic purposes, with no gain, benefits or notoriety accruing in return, as below.

Love your enemies and pray for those who persecute you, so that you may be children of your Father in heaven; for he makes his sun rise on the evil and on the good, and sends rain on the righteous and on the unrighteous. For if you love those who love you, what reward do you have? Do not even the tax collectors do the same? And if you greet only your brothers and sisters, what more are you doing than others....Be perfect, therefore, as your heavenly Father is perfect (Matthew 5:43-48, Luke 6:27-35).

Beware of practicing your piety before others in order to be seen by them; for then you have no reward from your Father in heaven (Matthew 6:1).

Do not judge, so that you may not be judged (Matthew 7:1, Luke 6:37).

Summarizing and focusing again on what Jesus emphasized for achieving the kingdom of heaven, He emphasized loving our neighbors as ourselves, living by the golden rule, being magnanimous to those who ask of us, caring about the poor, the afflicted, the imprisoned, by acting and giving, not just remuneration from our abundance, but giving time, effort and love with self-sacrifice, to those from whom no love, return or remuneration is sought, quietly and without notoriety. This no doubt is what moved President Jefferson to write the following about Jesus:

Notwithstanding these disadvantages, a system of morals is presented to us which, if filled up in the true style and spirit of the rich fragments he left us, would be the most perfect and sublime that has ever been taught to man. The question of his being a member of the Godhead, or in direct communication with it, claimed for him by some of his followers, and denied by others, is foreign to the present view.

His moral doctrines, relating to kindred and friends, were more pure and perfect than those of the most correct of the philosophers...and they went far beyond both in inculcating universal philanthropy, not only to kindred and friends, to neighbors and countrymen, but to all mankind, gathering all into one family, under the bonds of love, charity, peace, common wants and common aids. A development of this head will evince the peculiar superiority of the system of Jesus over all others.

He pushed his scrutinies into the heart of man; erected his tribunal in the region of thought, and purified the waters of the fountainhead. He taught emphatically the doctrine of a future state, which was either doubted or disbelieved by the Jews; and wielded it with efficacy as an important incentive, supplementary to the other motives to moral conduct.

Chapter 7.

THE LORD'S PRAYER

Considering the importance of the Lord's Prayer to Christian worship and the frequency with which it is recited, it can become a rote and meaningless recitation. Even when the words of the Lord's Prayer are given their common meaning, relatively little thought may be given to the implications, or the obligations the words of the Lord's Prayer impose. Significantly, the recitation of The Lord's Prayer is essentially a summary of the faithful practice of the Christian faith.

In today's Christian world the Lord's Prayer is not recited as it appears in scripture. The prayer as related by Jesus in Matthew and Luke is set forth below, verse by verse for purposes of comparison:

Matthew 6:9-13	**Luke 11:2-4**
9. Our Father in heaven, hallowed be your name.	2. Father, hallowed be your name.
10. Your kingdom come, your will be done, on earth as it is in heaven.	Your Kingdom come

11. Give us this day our daily bread.	3. Give us each day our daily bread.
12. And forgive us our debts, as we also have forgiven our debtors.	4. And forgive us our sins, for we ourselves forgive everyone who is indebted to us.
13. And do not bring us to the time of trial, but rescue us from the evil one.	And do not bring us to the time of trial.

Certainly, the exact wording Jesus gave his disciples is unknown. The translations from the ancient Greek are the best we have. The Matthew version of the Lord's Prayer is the basis for our present-day Lord's Prayer shown below:

Our Father, who art in heaven,

hallowed by Thy name.

Thy kingdom come, Thy will be done

on earth as it is in heaven.

Give us this day our daily bread.

And forgive us our trespasses,

as we forgive those, who trespassed against us.

And lead us not into temptation,

But deliver us from evil.

For Thine is the kingdom and the power and the

glory forever. Amen.

The Lord's Prayer does not appear in Mark, John, the writings of Paul, or in any other letters or books of the Bible. In terms of the context in which it was presented, the Matthew version of the Lord's Prayer was a part of the Sermon on the Mount. It was preceded by an instruction from Jesus on how to pray to avoid hypocrisy (Matthew 6:1-9). The Luke version of the Lord's Prayer was presented by Jesus after an unidentified disciple asked Jesus to teach them how John the Baptist taught his disciples to pray (Luke 11:1-8).

The phrasing in Matthew, *"Thy kingdom come, Thy will be done, on earth as it is in heaven,"* raises questions when compared to the Luke version which only states, *"Thy kingdom come."* One could be excused for believing that God's kingdom incorporates God's will, and that God's will is an inherent part of, and inseparable from God's kingdom. Luke's version supports the interpretation that God's will is inherently a part of God's kingdom. For purposes of Christian prayer life, it may not matter how this phrase of the prayer is recited.

The words, *"Thy kingdom come,"* or *"Thy kingdom come, Thy will be done, on earth as it is in heaven,"* create an obligation for believers whose faith is manifested in faith-based works to arrange their lives, resources, priorities and actions to conduct their life on earth in accordance with Jesus' examples and teachings as set forth in the previous chapter. This interpretation is supported by the next sentence, *"Give us this day our daily bread."* The prayer for daily bread, sustenance from God, cannot be one that allows believers to receive this sustenance, and then live lives oblivious to God's purposes of justice, the needs of the afflicted, the sick, the hungry, the poor, or the imprisoned.

For believers in faith-based works, *"Thy kingdom come, Thy will be done, on earth as it is in heaven. Give us our daily bread"* creates a personal covenant with God. We ask that God provide our daily bread so that we can strive to live our lives in accordance with Jesus' teachings and examples. For believers in justification by faith alone, acceptance of Jesus as Lord and Savior would apparently create this personal covenant.

The next phrase in the prayer is *"forgive our debts, as we forgive our debtors,"* or *"forgive our trespasses, as we forgive those who trespassed against us."* Many persons will fail to recognize that the debts and trespasses requested to be forgiven include the failure to live our lives in accordance with Jesus' teachings and examples. For many, the lack of complete dedication in living our lives in accordance with

Jesus' teachings and examples is likely to be the greatest of all debts or trespasses needing forgiveness. For believers in justification by faith alone, asking for forgiveness of debts and trespassed would result in a more limited request for forgiveness.

Just as you did it to one of the least of these who are members of my family, you did it to me.

> "Come you that are blessed by my Father, inherit the kingdom prepared for you from the foundation of the world; for I was hungry and you gave me food, I was thirsty and you gave me something to drink, I was a stranger and you welcomed me, I was naked and you gave me clothing, I was sick and you took care of me, I was in prison and you visited me."…Then the righteous will answer him, "Lord, when was it that we saw you hungry and gave you food, or thirsty and gave you something to drink? And when was it we saw you a stranger and welcomed you, or naked and gave you clothing? And when was it that we saw you sick or in prison and visited you?" And the king will answer them, "Truly I tell you, just as you did it to one of the least of these who are members of my family, you did it to me" (Matthew 25:34-40).

Just as you did it to one of the least of these who are members of my family, you did it to me. In today's complex world we need to be more aware of our actual debts and trespasses. Acting in a careless, thoughtless or politically ignorant manner does not excuse our debts or trespasses. The covenant created by the Lord's Prayer allows the forgiveness of our debts and trespasses so long as we forgive the debts and trespasses of others against us.

The Lord's Prayer next states, *"And lead us not into temptation."* To avoid focusing on God leading them into temptation, some interpret the prayer as not allowing the prayer to be led by others, or Satan, into temptation. However, this is the Lord's Prayer. Believers are praying to God, and are asking God, not Satan or others, to not lead them into temptation. Regarding temptation, James 1:13-14 states, *"No one, when tempted, should say, 'I am being tempted by God'; for God cannot be tempted by evil and he himself tempts no one. But one is tempted by one's own desire..."* Contrary to James, God used Satan to tempt Job (Job 1:9-13).

Nevertheless, James has a point. The wording, *"Lead us not into temptation"* is difficult to interpret in a meaningful way. As noted above, the Lord's Prayer in its presently recited form has been changed from the versions in scripture. The words "temptation" and "trial" are derived from the same Greek word. The prayer in both Matthew and Luke is, *"And do not bring us to the time of trial,"* rather than, *"Lead us not into temptation."*

As previously stated, a review of scripture indicates that Jesus was fearful and overcome at Gethsemane when confronted with facing his destiny. Jesus knew he was facing betrayal, trial, crucifixion and death. He asked God that if it were possible, to let the cup pass from him; but that it should not be what [Jesus] wanted, but what God wanted (Matthew 26:36-46, Luke 22:39-46). Jesus bowed to God's will and went through with his arrest, trial and crucifixion. Jesus offered prayers and supplications, with loud cries and tears to the one who was able to save him from his death, Hebrews 5:7. He cried out on the cross asking why God had forsaken him, Mark 15:34, Matthew 27:45-50.

Jesus' words, *"My God, my God, why have you forsaken me?"* are the first words in Psalm 22, part of which is quoted below:

My God, my God, why have you forsaken me? Why are you so far from helping me, from the words of my groaning? O my God, I cry by day, but you do not answer, and by night, but find no rest (Psalm 22:1-2).

While at Gethsemane:

> He [Jesus] took with him Peter and the two sons of Zebedee, and began to be grieved and agitated. Then he said to them, "I am deeply grieved, even to death; remain here and stay awake with me." And going a little farther, he threw himself on the ground and prayed, "My Father, if it is possible, let this cup pass from me; yet not what I want but what you want." Then he came to the disciples and found them sleeping; and he said to Peter, "So, could you not stay awake with me one hour? Stay awake and pray that you may not come into the time of trial" (Matthew 26:37-41, Mark 14:33-37, Luke 22:40-46).

Matthew and Luke are the gospels that contain The Lord's Prayer. Thus, Jesus' directing his disciples to *"Pray that you may not come into the time of trial"* is relevant here. The disciples would not have fully understood what Jesus meant by this part of the prayer until after Jesus' crucifixion, resurrection and appearances. However, it is likely that Jesus had this in mind, when instructing his disciples how to pray, knowing that he would soon no longer be with them.

Praying that we do not come into the time of trial is a reminder of Jesus being betrayed, his trial, and his public crucifixion that included concerns that God had abandoned him. *"Lead us not into temptation"*; probably not. The words in the Lord's Prayer should be what are in the scriptures; *"And do not bring us to the time of trial."* Jesus set an example of obedience to God for us. When we pray "bring us not to our time of trial" we are reminded of Jesus' betrayal, trial, and crucifixion, and we are asking God to save us from such a trial and uncertainty.

The last phrase of the Matthew version of The Lord's Prayer is, *"but rescue us from the evil one."* Luke's version has no corresponding wording. The Lord's Prayer recited in churches today sets forth the last phrase as *"But deliver us from evil."* Scholars differ as to whether "evil" refers to "evil" in general, or to the "evil one," as in the Matthew version of the prayers. The phrase, *"But deliver us from evil"* can mean to protect the prayer from evil. It can also mean that the prayer does not become the perpetrator of evil. Humans frequently are the perpetrators of evil either intentionally or unwittingly. The Lord's Prayer in the scriptures does not include a doxology.

As stated above, the recitation of the Lord's Prayer is essentially a summary of the faithful practice of the Christian faith. It creates a covenant to bring God's kingdom in the form of a more perfect existence to this earth. We are praying for our daily bread, the sustenance needed to bring God's kingdom to earth. We are praying that God forgive our debts or trespasses, confessing our lack of self-sacrifice and dedication in bringing God's kingdom to earth. We are also confessing our lack of awareness of how, in this complex world, we are ignorantly of unwittingly trespassing and incurring debts against others.

Who is doing the will of the Father's in heaven in today's world? Who are today's Christian heretics?

Chapter 8.

CHURCHES TODAY: PROMOTING SALVATION?

The primary mission of churches, as it has always been, is to lead their members to salvation. Leading their members to salvation means preaching God's message as conveyed by Jesus. Many churches have supplanted or obfuscated Jesus' mission with Paul's message; accepting Jesus as our Lord and Savior, because Jesus died for our sins. There is a significant difference between God's message, as preached and demonstrated by Jesus, and Paul's message limited to Jesus' crucifixion and resurrection.

Many church leaders having focused on their studies in theological colleges and seminaries generally lack the broader knowledge, education, training and experience to cogently address the moral and ethical issues in today's world. They also lack the inclination, because of the potential divisiveness these issues may cause within their congregations. Jesus didn't shy away from presenting divisive issues.

Christian seminaries need to better address what it means to love our neighbors in the context of the today's materialism, gun violence, political corruption, the impact of growing income disparity, the plight of the poor and the imprisoned, the impact of pollution on health and longevity, the degradation of our environment, our endless wars and killings, etc. We treat our immediate family members well most of the time. However, we give little thought to the frequently unknown or unforeseen, but nevertheless devastating impacts of our political activities, or to our lack of political activities. We frequently forget that Jesus said:

> Love your enemies and pray for those who persecute you, so that you may be children of your Father in heaven; for he makes his sun rise on the evil and on the good, and sends rain on the righteous and on the unrighteous. For if you love those who love you, what reward do you have? Do not even the tax collectors do the same? And if you greet only your brothers and sisters, what more are you doing than others?...Be perfect, therefore, as your heavenly Father is perfect (Matthew 5:44-48, Luke 6:27-36).

The god presented in many of today's churches pays little regard to the obligations of church members to endure self-sacrifice to serve the poor, the displaced, the afflicted, and the imprisoned, beyond those we love and who love us. Jesus' life on earth was an example of the deprivation and self-sacrifice in conveying God's message and doing God's work. What Jesus emphasized for salvation was loving our neighbors as ourselves, living by the golden rule, being magnanimous to those who ask of us, caring about the poor, the afflicted, the imprisoned, by acting and giving, not just remuneration from our abundance, but giving time, effort and love with self-sacrifice, to those from whom no love, return or remuneration is sought, quietly and without notoriety. Jesus message has been lost by many in today's Christianity.

In a column for the *Washington Post*, Colbert I. King explored the question of what is a Christian. He noted that the Reverend Martin Luther

King expressed disappointment in his 1963, *Letter From Birmingham Jail*, that in the midst of blatant racial and economic injustices, most white ministers remained silent behind the anesthetizing security of their stained glass windows. Reverend King spoke of traveling and looking at the South's beautiful churches with their lofty spires pointing heavenward, and wondering what kind of people worshipped there, and who their God was. One of Colbert King's conclusions was that:

> It appears that Christians are just as adept at interpreting the Bible to suit their political and personal beliefs as radical Islamists who twist the Koran to suit theirs.

When viewed from the Christian perspective of loving thy neighbor, many of today's churches are spawning members who appear to be following a self-centered, self-righteous perspective that is absent of love, but abundant in being judgmental of others. Strongly opinionated, self-righteous Christians generally have incurred little or no self-sacrifice for the betterment of humanity. Generally, they have not walked in the shoes of the persons they sit in judgment of. To the extent they may be driven by altruistic motives in their self-righteousness they have forgotten Jesus' admonition:

> Do not judge, so that you may not be judged. For with the judgment you make you will be judged, and the measure you give will be the measure you get. Why do you see the speck in your neighbor's eye, but do not notice the log in your own eye? Or how can you say to your neighbor, "let me take the speck out of your eye," while the log is in your own eye? You hypocrite, first take the log out of your own eye, and then you will see clearly to take the speck out of your neighbor's eye (Matthew 7:1-5).

The message in James' letter to the early church has largely been lost:

Be doers of the word, not merely hearers who deceive themselves. For if any are hearers of the word and not doers, they are like those who look in the mirror; for they look at themselves and, on going away, immediately forget what they were like. But those who look into the perfect law, the law of liberty, and persevere, being not hearers who forget, but doers who act—they will be blessed in their doing...(James 1:22-25).

What good is it, my brothers and sisters, if you say you have faith but do not have works? Can faith save you? If a brother or sister is naked and lacks daily food, and one of you says to them, "Go in peace; keep warm and eat your fill," and yet you do not supply their bodily needs, what is the good of that? So faith by itself if it has no works is dead...(James 2:14-17).

Was not our ancestor Abraham justified by works when he offered his son, Isaac on the altar? You see that faith was active along with his works....Thus the scripture was fulfilled that says, "Abraham believed God, and it was reckoned to him as righteousness," and he was called the friend of God. You see that a person is justified by works and not be faith alone (James 2:21-24).

As previously stated, the society Jesus was born into was basically agrarian; comprised primarily of farmers, fishermen, carpenters, blacksmiths and other tradesmen. There were no transnational corporations that could transfer manufacturing or entire industries to foreign lands leaving segments of the local population unemployed and poor. There were no rapid changes in technology, automation or robotics that could displace large segments of peoples' livelihoods.

This is not the same world. These are not the same circumstances. We are not the same people as the people who lived in Jesus' time more than 2,000 years ago. There was no concern about nuclear and chemical weapons, biological warfare, cyber-warfare, water and air pollution, climate change, overpopulation, artificial intelligence, and the extinction of essential species because of human activities. Jesus' concerns for the poor, the afflicted, the imprisoned and the less fortunate certainly exist today, but they are on a massive, systemic and international scale.

The worsening concentration of wealth is an example of the poor, the impoverished and the deprived on a systemic scale. Certainly, individual actions and examples are much needed. However, we must also adapt Jesus' teachings to today's world, reform our government, and act through our government to address these issues. Free markets and capitalism have certain advantages, but they have also gotten us to where we are today.

As a nation we continue to gravitate towards a government corrupted by greed, materialism, wealth and undue influence. We continue on our path to a greater concentration of wealth. We continue to be in a state of perpetual war and killings. We do business with countries who buy weapons, services and products from us, though they oppress their citizens worse than our alleged enemies. We continue to have the largest prison population in the world. We continue to have the greatest number of domestic killings in the in the world. We continue to incur a larger national debt to the detriment of our children, grandchildren and our posterity.

We continue to head towards the insolvency of Social Security, Medicare and Medicaid when our children and grandchildren will need them. We continue to pay almost double what other citizens of advanced nations pay for health care, while experiencing a lower and worsening life expectancy and greater infant mortality than other advanced nations. We continue to abuse our planet and do next to nothing to at least slow global warming and climate change, at the expense of our children, grandchildren and posterity.

We have gotten to this state of affairs because we live in a society in which too many Christians are motivated by the non-Christian values of materialism, greed and power. We are not living by the commandment to love our neighbor as ourselves. We are not living in accordance with the golden rule. We do not show magnanimity towards the needs of others. These are not easy requirements to live by. However, these were among Jesus' profound requirements:

> You shall love the Lord your God with all your heart, and with all your soul, and with all your mind. This is the greatest and first commandment. And a second is like it: You shall love your neighbor as yourself. On these two commandments hang all the law and the prophets (Matthew 22:37-40, Mark 12:30-33).

Jesus said, *"Beware of false profits, who come to you in sheep's clothing, but inwardly are ravenous wolves"* (Matthew 7:15). We've apparently regressed to a more subtle calling than that of Jim and Tammy Faye Bakker and the PTL Club. Many of today's preachers are more business and politically astute and have learned the lessons of networking and better business marketing.

The pious participants of the annual National Prayer Breakfast and its surrounding events, *"has become an international influence peddling bazaar, where foreign dignitaries, religious leaders, diplomats and lobbyists jockey for access to the highest reaches of American power,"* according to *New York Times* journalists Kenneth Vogel and Elizabeth Dias. Jeffery Sharlet, a Dartmouth College associate professor of journalism in his book, *The Family: The Secret Fundamentalism at the Heart of American Power* described "the Fellowship" as an organization that uses the National Prayer Breakfast and surrounding events as a means of recruiting and promoting contact between lobbyists and foreign governments, using the image of Jesus as a strongman who gets things accomplished without any government oversight.

Today, the United Nations Refugee Agency states there are 70,000,000 million forcibly displaced persons and refugees in the world: more than during World War I and World War II. Are we doing all we can for them? Indeed, are we doing very much at all? Pope Francis doesn't think so. Are the churches doing much to combat the racism and intolerance generated against the persons displaced? Or are many churches, if by nothing more than offering their silence, condoning the hatred, intolerance and indifference?

Pope Francis stated that choosing *"to not see hunger, disease, exploited persons, this is a grave sin. It's also a modern sin of today."* Pope Francis also denounced as scandalous the amounts of money governments and world institutions have found to save ailing banks, but not suffering people including migrants who are drowning and dying as they try to cross the Mediterranean Sea. He criticized these policies as indicative of the bankruptcy of humanity. Do church members and their clergy have no stake in what's happening? Is their salvation really assured?

Regarding salvation being based on more than just faith in Jesus, Jesus says, *"Enter through the narrow gate; for the gate is wide and the road is easy that leads to destruction, and there are many who take it. For the gate is narrow and the road is hard that leads to life, and there are few who find it"* (Matthew 7:13-14). *"...Not everyone who says to me 'Lord, Lord' will enter the kingdom of heaven, but only the one who does the will of my Father in heaven. On that day many will say to me 'Lord, Lord, did we not prophesy in your name, and cast out demons in your name, and do many deeds of power in your name?' Then I will declare to them, 'I never knew you, go away from me you evildoer'"* (Matthew 7:21-23).

In Jesus' world it was much easier to see who might be injured by our individual actions. Generally, there was a direct causal connection. We have not adapted Jesus message to today's world. In today's world, we need to become more aware of the distant repercussions of the operations of our government, who we vote for, what our politicians really support, and the impact on other persons. In today's world salvation is much more difficult to achieve than many of today's churches lead their followers to believe. It is up to each of us to redirect our lives to achieve these goals

Who is doing the will of the Father in heaven in today's world? Who are today's Christian heretics?

Chapter 9.

ORIGINALISM: UNDERMINING DEMOCRACY?

Background

Followers of conservative and libertarian judicial philosophy introduced the concept for the interpretation of the Constitution known as "originalism." As this concept relates to the Constitution, an *originalist*, that is a judge or justice of the Supreme Court, or a person who believes in originalism, would interpret the Constitution in accordance with the intentions of those who originally drafted it, though their intentions are unknown. There is no evidence that the original drafters of the Constitution ever thought of, let alone advocated the concept of originalism. Moreover, how the original drafters would have interpreted the Constitution is now in the hands of activist-advocates who can't give the original drafters the benefit of the enlightenment of the concepts and issues that didn't exist and were never considered by the original drafters. Originalists insist originalism will curb so-called liberal judges from deciding cases that expand rights allegedly not in the Constitution, such as same sex marriage, contraception, abortion and even voting. While these are being curbed, originalists are advancing concepts that would have been anathema to the original drafters such as freedom of speech and freedom of religion for corporations and anonymous entities.

More than fifty delegates from twelve states attended the Constitutional Convention in Philadelphia where the Constitution was drafted. The delegates' drafting effort was a common effort headed by Alexander Hamilton that was completed September 17, 1787. Article VII of the draft provided that ratification by nine states was sufficient for establishment of the Constitution among the states ratifying it. On December 7, 1787, Delaware was the first state to ratify the Constitution. On June 21, 1788, New Hampshire was the ninth state to ratify thereby officially establishing the Constitution among the ratifying states. The delegates who drafted the Constitution never expressed an intention regarding how the Constitution should be interpreted, except in the Preamble to the Constitution that is set forth and discussed below. Ironically, the Preamble is largely ignored by originalists.

In the meantime, there was considerable opposition within the state of New York to ratification. To counter this opposition Alexander Hamilton, James Madison and John Hay collaborated to draft a series of 85 papers advocating ratification. The papers became known as the Federalist Papers. Though Federalist Paper 78 advocates *"judicial restraint,"* it is not a part of the Constitution. Significantly, the Federalist Papers were published primarily in New York newspapers after the Constitution was drafted. Thus, often cited as supporting *originalism*, the Federalist Papers had no effect on drafting the Constitution, or on any theory of interpretation. On July 26, 1788, New York became the eleventh state to ratify.

The concept of originalism could be relevant for purposes of interpreting the intentions of the single drafter of a will likely to soon be probated. However, it is irrelevant for purposes of determining the intentions of the more than 50 delegate drafters of the Constitution from twelve states whose intent was to guide the activities of a new government into perpetuity, and protect the interests of their particular state that at the time included slavery.

The Federalist Society, organized, promoted and well financed by conservative and libertarian organizers and fund raisers came into being in 1982. It promotes the concept of judicial restraint and many of its members and followers are originalists. Its website, https://fedsoc. org, describes itself as an organization of:

> conservatives and libertarians dedicated to reforming the current legal order, [and that it is] *emphatically the province of the judiciary to say what the law is, not what it should be …*

The Federalist Society has been operated as a 501(c) (3), non-profit, tax-exempt, organization since its founding in 1982. Under IRS regulations, https://www.irs.gov/charities-non-profits,

> To be tax-exempt…an organization must be organized and operated exclusively for exempt purposes.…In addition, it may not…attempt to influence legislation as a substantial part of its activities… Organizations described in section 501(c) (3) are commonly referred to as charitable organizations…eligible to receive tax-deductible contributions…Section 501 (c) (3) organizations are restricted in how much political and legislative (lobbying) activities they may conduct.

Regarding the impartiality of the Federalist Society and the judges it promotes, it is essential to understand its fund-raising activities. A *Washington Post* article, dated May 22, 2019, entitled, *"The activist behind the push to reshape U.S. courts,"* was written by Robert O'Harrow, Jr. and Shawn Boberg. It details the fund-raising and other activities of the Federalist Society, and its Executive Vice President, Leonard Leo, the president's unofficial judicial advisor. The article reported that Leo, a devout Catholic driven by his faith and a literal [originalist] interpretation of the Constitution, has been on a two decade:

> mission to turn back the clock to a time before the U.S. Supreme Court routinely expanded the government's authority and endorsed new rights such as abortion and same-sex marriage... The story of Leo's rise offers an inside look into the modern machinery of political persuasion. It shows how undisclosed interests outside the government are harnessing the nation's nonprofit system to influence judicial appointments that will shape the nation for decades. Even as Leo counseled [the President]...he and his allies were raising money for nonprofits that under IRS rules do not have to disclose their donors. Between 2014 and 2017 alone, they collected more than $250 million in such donations, sometimes known as dark money... The money was used in part to support conservative policies and judges, through advertising and through funding for groups whose executives appear as television pundits.

In 1990, Leo...met Clarence Thomas, then an appellate judge. The two became close. With the election of George W. Bush, Leo began working as an outside advisor for the White House... among his allies was [Brett] Kavanaugh, then White House associate counsel.

In 2005 and 2006, Leo served as the leader of the campaigns supporting Supreme Court nominees John G. Roberts and Samuel

A. Alito. He and other members of the advocacy coalition spent about $15 million in donations from undisclosed donors on ads, telemarketing and the mobilization of "grass roots" groups... A key part of those efforts was a new nonprofit called the Judicial Confirmation Network, or JCN... One radio spot paid for by the JCN in Arkansas featured a local minister who warned listeners that liberals wanted to curb religious freedom, including Christmas celebrations.

Six of the nine justices on the Supreme Court are current or former members of the Federalist Society. The six also have Christian backgrounds, primarily Roman Catholic. They generally are the product of privileged Harvard and Yale educations. They very frequently form the five or six justice majority in the decisions described.

Though this Supreme Court professes to advocate judicial restraint, as set forth below, many of its decisions and rulings undermine the basic concepts of democracy and the separation of powers in the Constitution. The Federalist Society and this Supreme Court frequently disregard the language in the Constitution guaranteeing the individual rights of the people. The basic purpose of the Constitution as set forth in the Preamble is to, *"establish justice...promote the general Welfare...and secure the Blessings of Liberty."* Amendment IX provides, *"the enumeration of powers in the Constitution, of certain rights, shall not be construed to deny or disparage others retained by the people."* Amendment X provides, *"The powers not delegated to the United States by the Constitution, nor prohibited by it to the states, are reserved to the states, or to the people." There is no mention of corporate or anonymous entity rights, only rights of the people are protected as evidence by the Bill of Rights, the first ten amendments.*

As stated above, the Federalist Society came into being in 1982 with one of its primary purposes being: limiting judges to "saying what the law is, not what it should be." As that purpose is being implemented by this Federalist Society influenced Supreme Court, and as the cases below show, saying what the law is, appears to imposes forced arbitration, corrupts the electoral process, weakens individual rights and unionization, enhances corporate power and abuse, disenfranchises voters, and engrafts dictatorial powers into the presidency thereby undermining the Constitution.

Erosion of Personal Rights

Amendment VII to the Constitution provides that:

> In suits at common law, where the value in controversy shall exceed twenty dollars, the right to a trial by jury shall be preserved.

In AT&T Mobility vs. Concepcion (2011), Justice Scalia began the trend of eroding and eliminating consumers and worker rights against corporations. He authored the 5-4 Christian majority Federalist Society influenced Supreme Court decision overturning a California law that prevented arbitration clauses from restricting class action suits against corporations. To further the trend and notwithstanding Amendment VII to the Constitution, the Christian, Federalist Society influenced Supreme Court, in another 5-4 decision ruled that in lieu of court actions and other remedies to protect workers' rights, arbitration agreements can be imposed as a condition of employment on job applicants who would otherwise remain unemployed (Epic Systems vs. Lewis, 2018). The decision could affect millions of workers by eliminating their right to a trial by jury, concerted action, unionization and collective bargaining.

In deciding that individual workers can contract away their constitutional rights though dealing with the disparate power of multi-million dollar corporations, the court gutted the rights of workers to concerted action and unionization guaranteed under the National Labor Relations

Act. In deciding what the law is, the court essentially abolished the act of Congress; a long-standing labor relations law of the United States. When an individual job applicant or worker is pitted against a multi-million dollar corporation, the disparate bargaining power amounting to coercion essentially forces individuals to contract away their constitutional and statutory rights including class actions. Regarding class action suits, Judge Richard Posner of the U.S. Court of Appeals for the 7th Circuit, now retired, succinctly wrote that:

> The realistic alternative to a class action is not 17 million individual suits, but zero individual suits, as only a lunatic or a fanatic sues for $30.

Worker wage thefts occur when employers don't pay for overtime, require that work be done on workers' time, and fail to pay minimum wages. The National Employment Law Project estimated that $12.6 billion in worker wages were lost in 2019 as a result of arbitration clauses being imposed on workers. The Congress, the uninformed voters, and the Christian majority Federalist Society influenced Supreme Court are depriving individuals of their rights. Legislation and regulations are making it more difficult for patients and survivors of those who die or are injured by drug companies, medical device makers and hospitals to adequately recover for death, injuries, incapacities, and pain and suffering, or even out of pocket expenses. There are legislative movements to limit class actions, cap financial recovery of jury awards, limit punitive damages, and to change negligence and malpractice standards to make individual recovery more difficult.

Consumer agreements with business entities such as banks, cable and phone companies, credit card companies, airlines, car leasing companies and others frequently include fine print provisions precluding the individual from filing a lawsuit to settle a dispute. The fine print requires the person to settle the dispute through arbitration, sometimes by an arbitrator selected and paid for by the business entity. Class action suits in a court of law are precluded. The 2019 September/October *Public Citizen News* reported:

> Corporate apologists for arbitration often say it is an alternative venue to obtain justice. But in practice, it just means cheated or abused consumers, employees and others are out of luck. Forced arbitration confers blanket corporate immunity. A recent study from the American Association for Justice found that Americans are, literally, more likely to be hit by lightning than win a case when they are forced to arbitrate. On average, 382 consumers win cases in arbitration each year. Only 56 workers prevail every year.

The March 2020 *Consumer Reports* in its Clause for Concern reported:

> To be sure, you don't have to sign anything—or even click "*I agree*" on a website to be bound by arbitration. This clause can appear on product packaging or be buried deep in warranties, user manuals, or in [a website's] "*terms of use.*" Placing the clauses there, says, Myriam Gilles, a professor of law [at Cardoza Law School], is "*intended to obscure the immensity of the rights being forfeited.*"

Many consumer advocates believe arbitration is little more than a get-out-of-jail-free card for companies. "*The only objective of forced, pre-dispute, class-banning arbitration clauses*" is to deter small-dollar claims says professor Gilles. That plan seems to be paying off. An estimated 825 million consumer arbitration agreements were in force in 2018. Yet only about 7,000 arbitration cases are actually heard each year, according to a 2019 study by researchers at the University of California, Davis School of Law.

Corruption: Corporate Freedom of Speech?

In Citizens United v. Federal Election Commission (2010), a 5–4 decision, our Christian majority, Federalist Society influenced Supreme Court found that the bipartisan, 2002 McCain-Feingold, Campaign Finance Reform Act was unconstitutional, on the basis that political campaign spending limits imposed by the Act violated the free speech of corporations and anonymous donors.

Based on their experiences with the British corporations' colonist exploitation, the founding fathers viewed corporations with suspicion and limited their endeavors. Corporations never had free speech rights. Further, corporations are not citizens of our society. Corporations cannot vote or hold office. Their controlling interests could be in the hands of non-citizens whose interests conflict with the interests of voters. Nevertheless, the Court disregarded its former deference to the wisdom of Congress which regulated the dangerous effects of unfettered campaign finance spending when it enacted the Campaign Finance Reform Act.

Though bribing a politician for a single political favor used to be illegal, the Citizens United decision now allows corporations and anonymous donors to contribute millions of dollars to get politicians elected, to gain unlimited access over those politicians, thereby influencing and controlling those politicians during their entire term in office; not just for a single bill or action.

Today, this corporate freedom of speech of the wealthy and influential exercising undue influence is drowning out the speech of the powerless majority, while promoting political corruption, and perpetuating and accelerating the income and wealth disparity in the United States. Today, the originalist interpreters ignore conflicting colonial history and the Preamble to the Constitution which states that the underlying purpose of the Constitution is to, *"establish justice," "promote the general Welfare," "and secure the Blessings of Liberty to ourselves and our Posterity."*

Today, the originalist interpreters ignore Amendment IX, a part of the Bill of Rights to the Constitution, which provides: *"The enumeration in the Constitution, of certain rights, shall not be construed to deny or disparage others retained by the people."* Today, the originalist interpreters ignore Amendment X, also a part of the Bill of Rights of the Constitution, which provides: *"The powers not delegated to the United States by the Constitution, nor prohibited by it to the states, are reserved to the states respectively, or to the people."*

After ruling that corporations' free speech was violated when their political campaign spending was limited, our Supreme Court ruled that corporate free speech rights were also violated when a corporation was required to post notices to prevent pregnant women from being misled. California legislators concluded that the Crises Pregnancy Centers falsely claimed that they offered a full range of abortion services, when in fact many Centers were not staffed by medical professionals, and none advised women seeking advice about low-cost family-planning services offered by the state. A state law was enacted requiring the Centers to post notices about the state's services, and required unlicensed facilities to advise they did not provide medical services. In NIFLA vs. Becerra (2018) the Supreme Court in a 5-4 Christian majority, Federalist Society influenced decision concluded posting these notices violated corporate free speech.

By way of contrast Kentucky legislators passed a law directing doctors to perform an ultrasound on all pregnant women seeking abortions, even when not medically needed, to display the ultrasound and describe the images including organs and a heartbeat if present. Doctors who did not comply could be fined and referred to the state's medical-licensing board. The Supreme Court's Christian Majority, in a Federalist Society influenced 5-4 decision found that forcing doctors to perform unneeded ultrasounds and discuss the results did not violate doctors' free speech rights. The Supreme Court lesson is that doctors being forced to describe unneeded ultrasounds to pregnant women have inferior free speech rights under the Constitution than corporations misleading pregnant women (EMW Women's Surgical Center vs. Meier, 2019).

In deciding what the law is, rather than what the law should be, the Christian majority, Federalist Society influenced Supreme Court in a 5-4 decision granted religious freedom rights to a corporation at the expense of its employees (Burwell vs. Hobby Lobby, 2014). Hobby Lobby, a corporation with $4.3 billion in annual sales, claimed that its religious freedom was violated when it had to pay for women's birth control pills. Though federal law requires businesses to provide medical insurance for their employees, based on this Supreme Court precedent, a Jehovah Witness owned business could refuse to pay for blood transfusions. A Christian Science owned business could refuse to pay for any medical treatments.

Deference to States in Election Matters: Double Standards

Article II, Section 1, of the Constitution provides that, *"Each State shall appoint, in such a manner as the legislature thereof may direct, a number of electors ..."* Amendment X of the Constitution provides that *"The powers not delegated to the United States by the Constitution, nor prohibited by it to the states, are reserved to the states respectively, or to the people."* Articles I and Amendment X provide that state elections are managed exclusively by the states, not the federal government, least of all the Supreme Court. In the year 2000 presidential election the Florida state balloting indicated a close election between candidates George Bush and Albert Gore, with George Bush the slight winner.

Winning the Florida election would result in winning the national election. Because of the close election results and questions about how certain ballots were counted, the Florida Supreme Court ordered a total recount of all ballots.

Though there was no constitutional basis and no clear case precedent for intervening in the Florida Supreme Court's directed election recount, the Supreme Court in a 5-4 decision nevertheless intervened, holding the Florida Supreme Court's ordered recount unconstitutional, and essentially declaring George Bush president (Bush vs. Gore, 2000).

Justice Scalia was the leading edge of the originalist constitutional interpretation theorists on the Supreme Court. One of the basic principles of originalist interpretation is the preservation of states' rights. The fact that Justice Scalia and the Federalist Society influenced Supreme Court were advocates for protecting states' rights did not prevent them from sweeping aside Florida's state's rights when it served their purposes to do so. The fact that Justice Scalia was a duck hunting friend of George Bush's running mate, Vice President, Dick Cheney, might have played a role in Justice Scalia's decision to intervene. Indeed, if Justice Scalia had adhered to the judicial code of ethics which precludes participation in a case when even the appearance of a conflict of interest is present, Justice Scalia should have excluded himself from participating in the Court's decision. He did not do so.

When it suits its purposes, the court deviates from its mantra and decides what the law should be, rather than what the law is. For example, the Supreme Court held in favor of state rights, though gerrymandering disenfranchises millions of voters. Gerrymandering occurs when the political party in power draws the boundaries of state congressional districts to promote its own prospects of electing the largest number of representatives.

For example, Ohio was entitled to 16 congressional representatives in the 2018 election. There were approximately 2.2 million votes cast for Republican representatives and approximately 2 million for Democrat representatives. The 2.2 million Republican votes represented 52.3 percent of the 4.2 million total votes cast. The 52.3 percent would have entitled the Republicans to 52.3 percent of the 16 representatives; or 8.4 representatives. In order not to dismember a representative the Republicans were certainly entitled to nine of the 16 representatives. However, as a result of the Republican gerrymandered congressional districts, the Republicans were able to elect 12 of the 16 representatives; 75 percent of the total.

Were it not for the gerrymandered congressional districts, the four Democratic representatives could have been elected with only twenty-five percent of the total vote. Twenty-five percent of 4.2 million votes equals 1,050,000 votes. Since 2,000,000 Democrats voted, 950,000 Democratic voters were essentially disenfranchised by the gerrymandering (2,000,000 − 1,050,000 = 950,000).

Both parties engage in gerrymander and voters of all states are adversely affected. Gerrymandering should be prohibited because it disenfranchises voters and distorts the democratic process. Gerrymandering allows entrenched politicians to remain in office contrary to the desire of the majority. The Christian majority, Federalist Society influenced Supreme Court in its 5–4 decision refusing to find a basis to intervene in flagrant state gerrymandering found comfort in the fact that some form of gerrymandering was known to exist when the Constitution was ratified (Rucho vs. Common Cause, 2019). The proper response should have been: so did slavery, the oppression of Native Americans as savages, and the fact that women could not vote.

At the time of this Supreme Court decision two-thirds of the state legislatures were controlled by Republicans. This may have been a reason for the court majority's strange difficulty in finding a constitutional basis to intervene in state election gerrymandering, though it readily intervened in the Florida state election recount affecting the national election.

Notwithstanding there had been no evidence of election fraud, but for isolated cases, and the widespread history of discrimination against minority voters in a number of states, the Supreme Court struck down a portion of the 1965 Voting Rights Act dealing with those states discriminating against minority voters (Shelby County v. Holder 2013). This opened the door for those states as well as other states to increasingly enact laws restricting voting. These laws minimize the opportunities for mail-in voting, limiting the number of conveniently located ballot drop boxes, closing polls early and otherwise limiting the opportunity to vote.

An Arizona law required that ballots not be counted when legitimate voters cast the ballot in the wrong precinct, notwithstanding the fact that the precinct in which the ballot cast was closer or more convenient, or whether there was legitimate confusion because precincts had recently changed. The ballots would not be counted in total, even the votes for president, senator or representative that had nothing to do with precinct in which they were cast. The Arizona law also precluded anyone other than a member of the immediate household to carry in a ballot for an incapacitated voter. Those in the immediate household allowed included only a family member or caregiver. Excluded were neighbors, friends and relatives outside the household.

In the Democratic National Committee v. Brnovich, after considering the lower court ruling and the evidence of impact, the U.S. Court of Appeals for the Ninth Circuit found that these provisions unduly impacted Hispanics, Blacks and Native Americans. The court ordered that these provisions should not be enforced. Arizona appealed to the Supreme Court. Oral arguments were heard March 2, 2021. The questioning from the six member Federalist Society majority indicated it was inclined to reverse the Ninth Circuit and uphold the law notwithstanding its discriminatory effect. The trend is continuing. In 2021 there were 253 bills before state legislatures restricting voting rights.

Extraordinary Interference with Judicial Process

The Constitution established the Supreme Court as the court of last resort. Thus, the court generally does not intervene in cases that are not "ripe" for review. The ripeness of a case indicates the case has been fully and completely litigated in terms of the evidence presented, briefing and legal arguments, with a final decision from a lower court to review. In deciding what the law is, rather than what the law should be, the court has elected to intercede in cases not ripe for intervention, but where it has been politically expedient to do so. For example, before the Supreme Court's intervention, refugees could legally seek asylum in the United States so long as they did not pass through another country that could have granted safe asylum. The Attorney General (AG), contrary to the existing law, began restricting asylum to anyone who simply passed through another country, which essentially precluded any asylum from being granted. Further, the AG did so without complying with the Administrative Procedures Act (APA) which requires new rules to be published in the Federal Register for public notice and comment.

Thus, it was no surprise that a district court enjoined the AG's implementation of the new restrictions on asylum on the bases that the AG's actions were inconsistent with existing law, and because the AG failed to comply with the APA. The AG appealed to the U.S. Court of Appeals for the 9th Circuit, and while the case was in process and pending in the 9th Circuit, the AG appealed to the Supreme Court, which lifted the injunction (Barr v. East Bay Sanctuary Covenant, 2019). The Supreme Court's disregard for judicial restraint allowed the AG to disregard the law of asylum, and compliance with the APA. Most importantly, the court's action deprived asylum seekers the rights granted by Congress, and endangered the lives of those who could no longer seek asylum, contrary to U.S. immigration law.

In another example of the Supreme Court's premature intervention for political expediency, the administration had sought $5.7 billion for border wall construction. Congress appropriated $1.375 billion and limited construction to eastern Texas. Section 8005 of the Defense Appropriations Act allowed a transfer of funds within DOD appropriations for *"unforeseen military requirements"* and so long as the funds had not been requested and *"denied by Congress."* The administration declared an emergency to divert $2.5 billion in defense funds to construct the wall in New Mexico, Arizona and California to help in *"combating the enormous flow of illegal narcotics."* The Sierra Club sued to enjoin the construction on the basis of the irreparable harm to localities where the law would be built.

Again, not surprisingly, a district court granted the injunction holding that by the administration's own admission the need for the wall was not an *"unforeseen military requirement,"* and that the congressional refusal to grant the administration's funding request was a denial by Congress. On appeal, the 9th Circuit affirmed the injunction, and further cited Article I, Section 9, Clause 7 of the Constitution that *"No money shall be drawn from the Treasury but in consequence of appropriations made by law,"* as another reason to deny the administration's appeal. The $2.5 billion sought by the administration had not been appropriated by Congress. The 9th Circuit set a schedule to decide the case on the merits. In the meantime the administration appealed to the Supreme Court while the 9th Circuit case was pending. The Supreme Court prematurely accepted jurisdiction and lifted the injunction, Trump vs. Sierra Club (July 2019).

The court's lifting the injunction, notwithstanding the pending litigation in the 9th Circuit, had the effect of allowing the administration to divert $2.5 billion not appropriated by Congress for the border wall construction, and away from the other needs for which Congress had appropriated the money. The court's intervention allowed the administration to violate Section 8005 of the Defense Appropriation Act allowing funds to be diverted only for an unforeseen military emergency. The court's granting the stay resulted in the violation of Constitution Article I, Section 9, Clause 7 of the Constitution, cited by the 9th Circuit that *"No money shall be drawn from the Treasury but in consequence of appropriations made by law."* It also precluded proof of the irreparable harm the Sierra Club was prepared to show that the wall construction would destroy communities, public lands and waters in California, Arizona and New Mexico.

The court explained that district court judges issuing injunctions with nationwide impacts were wielding too much power. However, that power and authority is precisely what district courts are empowered to do to prevent irreparable harm, government injustices, and enforce the Constitution's separation of powers requirements. Further, the Supreme Court's interventions were not simply with the district court's actions, but while the case was pending before a circuit court that had upheld the propriety of the injunction. The Federalist Society influenced Supreme Court is undermining our very democracy when it ignores the fact that it is the Executive Branch that is wielding too much power by causing irreparable harm, violating our laws and undermining the Constitution's separation of powers, rather than the district courts wielding too much power. Justice Sonia Sotomayor expressed her disappointment with the administration in a less than forceful dissent from the court's premature intervention in another case when she stated:

> Claiming one emergency after another, the Government has recently sought stays in an unprecedented number of cases, demanding immediate attention and consuming limited court resources in each....and with each successive application, of course, its cries of urgency ring increasingly hollow.

In yet another example of its failure to exercise judicial restraint for the sake of political expediency, the New York State AG and the House Intelligence and Financial Services Committees were seeking release of the president's financial records from Capital One and Duetsche Bank. The AG was investigating alleged fraud, and the Committees were investigating foreign influence in U.S. elections. On appeals the U.S. Court of Appeals for the 2nd Circuit, and the District of Columbia Circuit Court of Appeals granted the AG's and the congressional committees' requests.

The circuit courts denied the president's requests to withhold the information, because the release could be accomplished without the president's effort, since the information sought was in the custody of Capital One and Deutsche Bank. The administration appealed to the Supreme Court to prevent the releases, and was granted a temporary stay. The Supreme Court later accepted the cases for review, delaying disclosure of the required information, but then failed to set an accelerated schedule for a decision.

By not setting an accelerated schedule for a decision, the Supreme Court granted the executive branch of government a significant victory by delaying the case brought by congressional committees seeking access to the president's financial records; even where those records were already in the custody of a third party. It might be understandable that the court would decide to hear the cases rather than allow the lower court decisions to stand, because of the separation of powers issues. However, as with the administration's many requests for lifting injunctions imposed against it, or when the operations of government can be seriously affected, or a presidency is at stake as in Bush v. Gore (2000), the court has shown it can render a decision within days.

By failing to set an accelerated schedule in these cases, the court delayed resolution of the cases until mid-2020, which in turn could delay consideration and resolution of the matters by the affected congressional committees, rendering their work of investigating foreign influence in U.S. elections useless. The court should not be intervening in cases in a manner that adversely impacts the work of Congress, a co-equal branch of government. The court's delay could impact the 2020 election. The court should not be delaying and deciding cases that will become moot.

In conclusion, regarding the Supreme Court, Senator Sheldon Whitehouse of Rhode Island writes:

> Chief Justice John G. Roberts Jr.'s insistence that his Court is above politics is belied by the array of 5-4 partisan decisions helping Republicans at the polls and big business elsewhere. At the polls, 5-4 partisan decisions helped Republicans gerry-mander, helped Republican legislatures suppress Democratic leaning voters, and helped corporate money flood elections and boost Republican candidates.

> For big business, 5-4 partisan decisions helped corporations who harmed their employees, helped corporations facing class action suits, helped corporations against unions, helped cor-porations steer consumers into corporate-friendly mandatory arbitration and gave corporations religious rights superseding employee health care. And unlimited corporate money in elec-tions helps big industry seek influence.

> For specific industries, 5-4 partisan decisions helped gun manu-facturers avoid regulation and liability, helped insulate invest-ment bankers from fraud claims and helped fossil-fuel industry pollute. Republican Justices are even giving hints so big busi-ness can get certain cases up to the Court pronto.

> Judicial principles, even "conservative" ones, overrun on the court's road to these results. Many decisions upend a century or more of law and precedent. Top writers and scholars describe

the Roberts court as serving the Republican Party along partisan lines to achieve an ideological agenda. Studies show it to be the most pro-corporate court in modern history.

As stated above, the well-financed and well-connected Federalist Society came into being in the early 1980s with one of its primary purposes being limiting judges to *"say what the law is, not what it should be."* As that purpose is being implemented, *saying what the law is*, appears to deprive individuals of their rights, enhances corporate power, disenfranchises voters, promotes corporate malfeasance, and engrafts dictatorial powers into the presidency undermining the Constitution.

Chapter 10.

UNDUE INFLUENCE: THE CONCENTRATION OF WEALTH

*T*he *Captured Economy, How the Powerful Enrich Themselves*, by Brink Lindsey and Steve Teles, and *Captured, The Corporate Infiltration of American Democracy*, by Senator Sheldon Whitehouse, document that private individuals and corporations with vast wealth have moved into politics as never before. These entities have enormous funds to spend on political candidates of their choosing, or against their candidates' opponents, depending on the politicians' voting record and their voting proclivities.

James K. Galbraith, in the fold to his book, *The Predator State*, states that we have become:

> a corporate republic, bringing the methods and mentality of big business to public life; a coalition of lobbies, doing the bidding of clients in the oil, mineral, military, pharmaceutical, agribusiness, insurance and media industries; and a predator state, *intent not on reducing government but rather on diverting public cash into private hands.*

Government has become a forum for lobbyists and so-called think tanks, funded by the wealthy and influential exercising undue influence. The public is unaware of the insecticide, herbicide, rodent feces, or insect remains that impose health risks in the cereal we eat; or what is allowed while safeguarding corporate profits. The public is unaware of the level of air pollution that is tolerable if only a ten-year reduction in average life expectancy can be expected, or the level that is allowed that safeguards corporate welfare. Regulatory tradeoffs such as these shift the expenses of cleanup, illnesses, suffering, medical expenses, reduced life expectancies, and deaths from corporate coffers to the general public.

The undue influence frequently results in legislation and regulations that allow these harmful levels, and then limit the financial appropriations for the government agencies tasked with enforcing what little discretionary enforcement remains. The government agencies can't adequately enforce standards even of limited value in protecting the public when the agencies are controlled by political appointees bent on assisting the industries from which they came, and to which they will eventually return.

Even before the Food and Drug Administration (FDA) approves a drug, lobbying efforts are already under way to preclude lawsuits against pharmaceutical companies that developed the drug. The FDA is generally headed by a former pharmaceutical industry representative or consultant. After all, the company met the government's FDA compliance procedures though the industry had a huge say in establishing the standards and the compliance procedures. If we must allow lawsuits, let's preclude class actions, so that each disadvantaged person must seek their own recovery. These and other measures are being promoted and implemented by corporate and business interests to be enacted at the federal and state levels.

There is no facet of our democracy or everyday life that has remained untainted by the political pressure and undue influence. As set forth in the PREFACE, even many of our universities are conveying propaganda laced information favoring wealthy and influential interests. George Mason Law School, a part of the George Mason University public education system in Virginia, was renamed Antonin Scalia Law School at George Mason University, after receiving $30 million in private donations including from the Koch Foundation. The University received another $50 million to name 13 new faculty chairs from the Roust Trust. Matthew Barakat, *Associated Press* reporter, on NBC Channel 4, reported that after considerable obfuscation by the University, it was determined that donation agreements gave the Koch Foundation a say in hiring and firing some professors, and that the Roust Trust donation was given to *"promote the conservative principles of governance"*, in a publicly funded university no less.

Public Citizen, in its July–August 2019 issue published excerpts from a June 2019 report by Taylor Lincoln, Research Director for Public Citizen's Congress Watch Division. The report stated that George Washington University's Regulatory Studies Center (RSC):

> claims to be an unbiased purveyor of analyses on regulatory policy issues. In reality, it's a corporate funded, anti-regulatory lobbying organization masquerading as a neutral center of academic inquiry....RSC's writings often focus on environmental issues—such as opposing proposals to reduce pollution and combat the climate crises—that have material implications for Koch Industries, the petroleum giant primarily owned by brothers Charles and David Koch....The report found that: Between 2013 and 2018, 96% of public comments submitted to government agencies by RSC writers on specific regulatory proposals recommended less regulation...75% of public comments submitted by RSC in this period were authored by people with past or present ties to Koch-funded entities....Funders of the

RSC are not fully disclosed but records from other organizations and cryptic disclosures from the university indicate that its funders include the Charles Koch Foundation, the libertine Searle Freedom Trust foundation, the far-right Sarah Scaife Foundation, ExxonMobil foundation, along with anti-Regulatory business trade associations, including the U.S. Chamber of Commerce, the Business roundtable and the American Chemistry Council....Koch funding of university programs has roughly quadrupled in the past decade, to 60 million annually, and Koch now helps fund more than 50 university centers.

Public Citizen reported that 76 senior administration lawyers previously represented businesses in matters directly affecting the agencies they work for. Many other lawyers performed legal work for or lobbied on behalf British Petroleum, Ford Motor Company, Verizon, Koch Industries and others. Most agencies' appointees are staffed by persons with recent and significant ties to the industries they are in a position to regulate. Penalties and fines levied by the Justice Department against businesses for wrongdoing have dropped to a fraction of previous penalties and fines. Penalties and fines levied by the Environmental Protection Agency for pollution abatement violations have also dropped to a fraction of previous penalties and fines.

The Washington Post reported that Scott Pruitt, former head of the Environmental Protection Agency, started consulting for coal magnate, Joseph W. Craft III. After leaving the Interior Department, energy counselor, Vincent DeVito joined Cox Oil Offshore as its Executive Vice President and General Counsel. Joe Balash, Interior's Assistant Secretary for Land and Minerals Development reportedly was joining an oil company expanding operations on Alaska's North Slope. Downey Magallanes met with British Petroleum executives while Deputy Chief of Staff to the Secretary of the Department of the Interior, and then led an effort to reduce the size of two wilderness protected areas for possible energy development. She then left the government to join British Petroleum's government affairs group. Former Secretary of Defense, Jim Mattis, rejoined the board of directors at General Dynamics.

Fifteen of the 47 lawmakers serving on the House Finance or Senate Banking Committees in 2008 were hired by Wall Street and other financial industry firms. Seventeen of the 40 most senior staffers on these same committees took jobs with the likes of JPMorgan Chase, Citigroup, Goldman Sachs, and lobby and consulting groups. Former Treasury Secretaries Timothy Geithner and Jack Lew have been executives with private-equity businesses. Former SEC Commission Chair, Mary Shapiro has been on the Morgan Stanley board. Former House, Financial Services Committee Chair, Barney Frank served on the Signature Bank board. Former Senate Banking Chair, Christopher Dodd, joined the Arnold & Porter Law firm. Henry Paulson, the Secretary of the Treasury who was instrumental in enacting the 2008 Emergency Economic Bailout Act, granting a $700 billion gift to bail-out the financial industry from its own fraudulent practices, came from Goldman Sachs.

Certainly, we need experts from the private sector to provide advice and guide government actions, but these needs should not be a forum for graft, corruption or self-enrichment. The "revolving door" rules need to be revised to incentivize public service, rather than public deprivation. Government salaries and benefits should be set to attract this talent rather than incentivizing flight to the private sector. Revolving door regulations need to prevent revolving door deprivation and public abuse for the benefit of the wealthy and influential exercising undue influence.

Another example of undue influence and political corruption are the House of Representative rules allowing members to own stock and sit as a board member of the corporations and businesses they regulate; even ones not in their district. A New York representative sat on the board of an Australian pharmaceutical company as a major stockholder, while serving on a committee with jurisdiction over the pharmaceutical industry. The representative was heavily invested in the Australian company as were his friends and family. Immediately after the company CEO advised the representative that an experimental drug failed a trial, the representative's friends and family sold their shares. Besides gaining inside information, being a director-shareholder places the representative in a position of power outside the role of a representative. Certainly, rule changes are needed.

In a *Washington Post* article by Lawrence Summers, past president of Harvard University, and Treasury Secretary from 1999 to 2001, and Natasha Sarin, assistant professor of law at the University of Pennsylvania Law School, and assistant professor of finance at the Wharton School, the authors reported that the federal government could collect more revenue without raising tax rates or reducing tax deductions. The authors reported that the IRS is leaving trillions of dollars uncollected, because *"... there are powerful interests that want to maintain the system that facilitates [tax] evasion."* Below are relevant excerpts from the article indicating the inadequate IRS tax enforcement of corporations and high-income persons.

In 2011, more than 12% of individuals making $1 million or more were audited; [in 2018] only 3.2% were....At present, recipients of the earned income tax credit—all of whom have incomes below $50,000—are about as likely as those making $500,000 or more to be audited. Only 5% of taxpayers earning above $5 million are audited—even though IRS data demonstrates that an extra audit-hour spent on their returns raises $5,000 on average. Fewer than 1% of corporate returns were audited in 2018—even though corporate audits on average raised nearly $1 million in additional revenue.

When third party income reports exist to compare with individual tax returns, income is correctly reported more than 95% of the time. Almost all income of individuals making $200,000 or less gets reported this way. But without such substantiation, between 17% and 55% of income goes unreported and untaxed—and more than two-thirds of the income of those who earn $10 million or more falls into this category.

What is the potential [for better and more efficient tax collection]? We priced out a program this weekend....Every $1 that is spent would generate more than $11 in greater tax collection.

However, as the authors noted above, *"there are powerful interests that want to maintain the system that facilitates tax evasion."*

Sheldon Gary Adelson, now deceased, was the billionaire owner of the Las Vegas Sands Corporation, which owned the Marina Bay Sands in Singapore. Mr. Adelson reportedly contributed $112 million in 2018 to political candidates. The continued illegality of internet gambling helped the profitability of Mr. Sheldon's brick and mortar enterprises. Apparently, gambling in casinos is acceptable, though gambling over the internet is not.

Koch Industries' history of failing to account for extracted oil from tribal oil wells, to oil spills, and a poor worker safety record are well documented in *Kochland*, by Christopher Leonard; *Sons of Wichita; How the Koch Brothers Became America's Most Powerful and Private Dynasty* by Daniel Schulman; and *Dark Money; The Hidden History of the Billionaires Behind the Radical Right* by Jane Mayer. Billionaire industrialist Charles Koch and several hundred other wealthy and influential associates under the umbrella of Americans for Prosperity (AFP) and other organizations are politically active in furthering their interests.

Members of AFP supported alleged public interest groups and political candidates whose agendas include income tax cuts, tax benefits for corporations and businesses, reduced government regulation, relaxed pollution abatement, weaker unions and collective bargaining, narrowing the scope of legal liability, limiting damages that can be assessed against them, etc. They also support conservative and libertarian views through funding of hundreds of professors across scores of universities, who quietly promote AFP-Koch policies and interests.

The undue influence and political corruption is creating the concentration of wealth. There has always been a concentration of wealth, but it has not been as exacerbated or as extreme as the present, and it is continuing to worsen. It was more tolerated at one time because it was never so large or pronounced that persons in the lower income brackets lacked a realistic chance and expectation of bettering themselves, and their families' financial well-being. Well regarded studies have found that extreme concentrations of wealth have a negative impact on economic growth and the contentment of the population.

As stated in the PREFACE, the concentration of wealth that has resulted can be illustrated very simply. Though there were many more two-person working households in 2018 when compared to 1989, nevertheless the median household income for 2018 was only $63,517 compared to 1989 $57,059 adjusted for inflation in 1989, only about an 11% increase in the 29 years since 1989.

For the same period the DOW Jones Industrial Average (DJIA) increased from 2,753 at the close of 1989 to 23,062 at the close of 2018; about an 837% increase from 1989. Yes, the value of publicly traded corporations grew eight times faster than the household median income. The increased wealth generally benefitted large stockholders; not the workers. The value of privately held corporations and businesses grew even greater.

Economists, Gabriel Zucman and Emanuel Saez, at the University of California at Berkeley, report that the richest 400 Americans pay

23% of their income in taxes, a lower rate than the working and middle class pay. The concentration of wealth is worse than Zucman and Saez portray, because these are the 400 Americans who at least declared a portion of their incomes and paid taxes, unlike countless others who partially or totally sheltered their income and paid very little or no taxes.

The Washington Post reported a study by the Institute on Taxation and Economic Policy showing that 55 of the largest corporations paid no federal income tax on more than $40 billion in profits in 2020. Though 26 companies such as Nike, FedEx, and Dish Network have booked more than $77 billion in profits since 2018, they paid no income taxes, while receiving $5 billion in rebates. All these companies used legal means to reduce or eliminate their tax liability. They lobbied for such provisions as tax breaks for stock options given their chief executives, credits for research and experimentation, and write-offs for renewable energy and capital investments.

One of the studies' authors, Matthew Gardner stated that though everyone wants to see businesses make more long term investments in the United States and conduct more research here, the evidence indicates these provisions resulted in more cash being sent to shareholders while employees were laid off. Kimberly Clausing, Deputy Assistant Secretary for Tax Analysis at the Department of the Treasury, addressing the Senate Finance Committee, stated that wealthy nations generally raise three-percent of GDP through corporate taxes, the U.S raises only one-percent, and that before the pandemic, profits as a share of GDP were running twice as high as in the period 1980-2000.

The enactment of the 2017 Tax Cuts and Jobs Act benefitted corporations and the wealthy, while increasing the national debt for our children and grandchildren. Among many other benefits granted the wealthy, it reduced the corporate tax rate from 35 percent to 21 percent. The Washington Post reported on a Forbes study showing that as a result the number of billionaires increased by 660 persons in 2020 from 2,095 to 2,755. While the tax cuts were palmed off on the gullible and powerless public as a means to stimulate the economy by hiring more workers, a December 2020 study by the London School of Economics showed that tax cuts consistently benefit the wealthy.

The Kiplinger Letter of July 2019, reported on the massive, domestic unregulated, $15 trillion, shadow banking industry that makes up about 70% of the size of the entire United States economy. Though this shadow economy can cause severe depressions and foster the avoidance of taxation, it remains unregulated because of the wealth and influence of those who comprise it. The wealthy and influential have legions of well-paid lobbyists, think tanks, privately funded foundations, tax exempt non-profit organizations, anonymous groups and indebted politicians in their hire.

Federal Reserve Chairman, Jerome H. Powell, testifying before a Senate panel stated that workers' wages and salaries accounted for 66% of the year 2000 U.S. Gross Domestic Product (GDP) of $10.3 trillion, but only 62% of the 2018 U.S., GDP of $19.39 trillion. Thus, though the overall wealth in the U.S. almost doubled from 2000—2018, workers' wages and salaries share of the wealth shrank. Few workers would be surprised by this fact. Many of the wealthy elite in the upper one percent are quite happy about it.

Another indicia of the greater concentration of wealth is land ownership. In 2007 the top 100 landowners in the United States owned 27.2 million acres of land; about the same acreage as in the states of Maine and New Hampshire combined. Just 10 years later in 2017 the top 100 landowners owned 40.2 million acres of land; about equal to the same acreage as the states of Maine, New Hampshire, Massachusetts and Connecticut combined; a 48% increase in 10 years.

Another indicia of the concentration of wealth is that there are 40% fewer publicly listed corporations and businesses than 20 years ago.

The United States GDP doubled during that time frame. The greater concentration of wealth in an ever fewer number of publicly held corporations and businesses has resulted in fewer persons controlling ever larger publicly and now, privately owned businesses, without being as accountable to public shareholders or the public. Cargill, Koch Industries, Mars, Bechtel, U.S. Foods and Hobby Lobby are examples of privately-owned businesses with billions of dollars in annual sales. They and their owners can further their private interests, personal influence and goals, while sheltering their fortunes, assets and income in foundations, nonprofits, philanthropic organizations, privately funded think tanks, and shadowy associations and organizations.

Another reason for the increased concentration of wealth has been the lost influence of unions and the resulting lack of focus on worker benefits. While some union activities have not always been in the best long-term interests of their members, unions generally have helped to equalize the disparate bargaining power between corporations and workers. Corporate and business lobbying has resulted in many states banning union shops, and globalization and the internationalization of labor have made it more difficult to form unions. This in turn has caused wages to stagnate, again shifting wealth from workers to corporations and businesses. Steven Greenhouse, a former labor reporter for the *New York Times*, in an article for the *Washington Post* in, *Yes, America Is Rigged Against Workers*, writes:

> The United States is the only advanced industrial nation that doesn't have laws guaranteeing paid maternity leave. It is the only advanced economy that doesn't guarantee workers any vacation paid or unpaid, and the only developed country other than South Korea that doesn't guarantee paid sick days...the United States has the lowest minimum wage as a percentage of the median wage; just 34 percent, compared to 62 percent for France and 54 percent for Britain...there is overriding agree-

ment on the reason: labor unions are weaker in the United States than in other industrialized nations....The consequences are enormous, not only for wages and income inequality, but also for politics and policy making and for the many Americans who are mistreated at work....That's one reason the percentage [of non-union workers] who want to join a union has risen from 32 percent to 46 percent....But, this desire to unionize faces some daunting challenges....One study found that 57 percent of employers threatened to close operations when workers sought to unionize, while 47 percent threatened to cut wages or benefits and 34 percent fired union supporters during unionization drives....The diminishing power of unions and workers has skewed American politics, helping give billionaires and corporations inordinate sway over America's politics and policymaking. In the 2015–16 election, business outspent labor $3.4 billion to $213 million....All the nation's unions, taken together spend about $48 million a year for lobbying in Washington, while corporate America spends $3 billion.

An example of the difficulties unions face and the impact on workers not represented by unions can be seen in the Netflix produced, *The American Factory*, which won the 2020 Academy Award for best documentary.

Workers relying on employer pensions that don't materialize frequently result in workers needing public assistance. The Employee Retirement Income Security Act (ERISA) established standards for private pension plans and set up the Pension Benefit Guarantee Corporation (PBGC). Religious affiliated businesses' pension plans are not covered ERISA and the PBGC. When workers' pensions are endangered because corporate employers fail to adequately fund their worker pension and multiemployer pension programs, the PBGC generally allows workers' pensions to be cut or eliminated. The PBGC had $2.3 billion in its multiemployer insurance fund to cover insured liabilities of $56.2 billion at the close of the government's 2018 fiscal year. Unlike its actions when financial industry interests were at stake, Congress reluctantly intervenes, if at all, to assist the adversely affected workers.

Corporations and businesses generally find the money needed to pay their dividends, or to buy back their shares to increase the value of the stock for their shareholders. Reducing corporate owner and executive salaries is never considered when businesses fail to adequately fund worker pensions. Further, employers can raid their pension funds to finance early retirements. These PBGC financial deficiencies and the impact of severely reduced worker pensions need to be compared with the 2008 $700 billion bailout of the banking industry by the government. Since ERISA exempts religious affiliated businesses, workers working for religious affiliated business expecting pension benefits need to review the viability of their pension plans with their religious employers. Guaranteeing pensions is a misnomer for the PBGC.

The *Washington Post* article entitled, "It's Better to be Born Rich Than Naturally Gifted," portraying a study showing that only 24-percent of the persons with the highest genetic potential born in the low income bracket graduated from college, but that 27-percent with the lowest genetic potential from the highest income group graduated from college. The study showed that income disparity is destroying the United States as a meritocracy. The greater concentration of wealth reduces economic potential and growth by depriving the lower economic strata the opportunity to contribute and prosper. The undue influence and the concentration of wealth wastes human resources to everyone's disadvantage; except perhaps for the wealthy exercising undue influence.

As stated above, Jesus ministry has been relegated to near obscurity and insignificance by the Nicene form of Christianity developed by the Greco-Roman influenced church in Rome, centuries after Jesus ministry, and later by the Reformation that abolished the need for faith-based works. Nevertheless, it is the Nicene form of Christianity that is preached in today's churches, and practiced by Jesus' alleged followers. This has resulted in our downward spiral of greed and undue influence corrupting our democracy and resulting in our national debt, a worsening confiscatory concentration of wealth, and the exploitation of our large majority.

Who is doing the will of the Father in heaven in today's world? Who are today's Christian heretics?

Chapter 11.

THE TOBACCO INDUSTRY SETTLEMENT

The tobacco industry presents a historical example of the wealthy and influential exercising undue influence resulting in the government's failure to protect the public and eliminate or at least regulate the detrimental impact on the health, medical expenses, lost wages, human suffering and the premature deaths of millions of persons over a period of decades. Though historical, it is included here because of the millions of persons adversely affected, whose health, damaged earnings capacity, suffering, shortened life expectancy, and deaths over many decades have never been made whole.

This tragedy was perpetrated by the wealth and political influence of the tobacco industry. It no doubt resulted from the wanton and willful, negligent, and even criminal conduct of many of its owners and executives, though no criminal charges were brought against them. This tragedy was also perpetrated by politicians influenced by tobacco industry campaign donations and their desire for re-election superseding their obligations to adequately represent and protect the voters who elected them. In today's complex world, we need to better understand the implications, impacts and repercussions of our political support and activities, or our lack of political activities, on others. We need to become better educated and more aware of the implications and repercussions.

A court ordered tobacco industry advertisement highlighted the industries' adverse impact on the health effects of smoking.

Smoking kills an average, 1,200 American every day.

More people die every year from smoking than from murder, AIDS, suicide, drugs, car crashes, and alcohol, combined.

Smoking causes heart disease, emphysema, acute myeloid leukemia, and cancer of the mouth, esophagus, larynx, stomach, kidney, bladder, and pancreas.

Smoking also causes reduced fertility, low birth weight in newborns, and cancer of the cervix.

For decades the tobacco industry hid the fact that the industry knew that the nicotine in tobacco was not only addictive, but that the tobacco smoke caused cancer, heart disease, emphysema and other health issues. Because of the nicotine addiction, it was extremely difficult for anyone who became a smoker to stop smoking, even though his or her health and very life depended on smoking cessation. In the meantime, the industry reaped billions of dollars in profits. Also in the meantime, the public unknowingly subsidized the tobacco industry's profits by paying for smokers' increased medical expenses, lost wages, decreased life expectancy and deaths. The industry made vast amounts of political donations to maintain its status.

Ultimately, a number of states' attorney generals filed lawsuits against the industry to recover state Medicaid expenses related to the smoking illnesses and diseases. Related medical expenses covered by private insurers were not included. Congress and the Clinton administration offered a number of failed solutions that would cap damage award payments, increase the price of cigarettes, impose industry advertising restrictions, and provide relief to tobacco farmers, demonstrating congressional intent to protect the tobacco industry as its highest priority rather than the addicted public. A less than contrite tobacco industry called the proposed solutions punitive and patently unconstitutional. Federal legislation was not enacted. However, a Master Settlement Agreement (MSA) was reached by the attorney generals for 46 states with the largest four tobacco companies in 1998. Other states and other tobacco companies joined the agreement.

Along with the payment to the states for their Medicaid expenses, and payments for the future medical costs of caring for persons with smoking related illnesses, the tobacco companies agreed to limit certain tobacco advertising. The payments to some 46 states of $206 billion over 25 years was well within the industries' financial ability to pay, The MSA was justifiably criticized because little or no benefits accrued to the afflicted smokers, who would continue to suffer with their maladies, addictions and pay higher prices for their cigarettes, subsidizing the industries' payments to the states. Significantly, no industry executives were prosecuted for the illnesses, suffering and the premature deaths they caused, or for their roles in the cover up.

This is an example of an industry whose vast profits were knowingly derived by causing the addiction, sicknesses and premature deaths of millions of persons. The industry was large and influential enough to do what it did without criminal prosecutions being filed against its executives. Moreover, no executives were known to have lost their jobs or pay. Yet, we've imprisoned 2,000,000 of our citizens, many for more than seven years for as little as a $200 drug transaction.

Though smoking has been limited in indoor public spaces, smoking and secondhand smoke still kills almost 500,000 persons in the United States each year. Though the incidence of smoking has been reduced, we now have flavored E-cigarettes and vaping. E-cigarette smoke that exposes users and nearby persons to toxic and carcinogenic substances which have caused immediate hospitalization. How will our government deal with this new health threat? Will it protect our youth, or will it protect the profits that are partially recycled for re-elections that allow greed to flourish?

We hear today about too much government regulation that increases costs and allegedly kills jobs. In the case of the tobacco industry, millions of people experienced cancer, emphysema, heart disease and other illnesses, suffering, death, lost wages and family separations over many decades. They suffered and died because of the actions of the tobacco industry owners, executives and politicians who remained silent to protect the industry in exchange for campaign contributions and re-election support, and because of ignorant and uninformed voters. Those who were afflicted and died, and those who continue to suffer with their families, have never been made whole.

The undue influence and concentration of wealth that allowed the tobacco industry owners, executives and their captive politicians to thrive, while destroying the public's health, welfare and longevity, can't be allowed to infest and corrupt our democratic infrastructure, food safety, healthcare, climate change and environment, military-industrial-congressional complex, prison industry, banking and financial security, our inherent right to privacy, etc. That undue influence and concentration of wealth is much worse now than more than two decades ago.

Chapter 12.

FOOD SAFETY

The public frequently and unknowingly votes for political candidates that support lax standards in the amount of pesticides, herbicides, hormones, chemicals, additives and genetic modifications in our food supply. Few political candidates with a true public interest can survive the vetting process and the financial support by the corporate and business interests seeking to maintain their undue influence. As stated above, the issue can be about the safe percentage of insects, rodent parts or animal feces in our cereal. The process and procedure for sampling and inspecting for these impurities is more than ever generally being left up to the food producers, rather than government inspectors.

The producer costs for the sampling and inspection are passed down to the consuming public as an increased price of the food product. The increased cost is not seen as a tax, but that's precisely what it is. Adequately staffed FDA and USDA's, Food Safety and Inspection Service (FSIS) sponsored inspection services have been weakened, minimized or eliminated under the guise of reducing the size of government and taxes. How well are the industry inspections protecting the public?

An investigation by *Consumer Reports* found prohibited drugs in the beef, poultry and pork we eat. Among the drugs found were: Ketamine, a hallucinogenic and an experimental anti-depressant; Phenylbutazone, an anti-inflammatory too risky for human use; and Chloramphenicol, an antibiotic linked to deadly anemia. The data for these conclusions came from USDA's FSIS, the agency allegedly in charge of ensuring the safety of the country's meat supply.

FSIS, which is largely captive in its inspection efforts to the food industry it is supposed to be inspecting, insisted the results should be discounted because they came from "unconfirmed" screen tests, notwithstanding the fact that the data originated with FSIS. A microbiologist for Consumers stated that he *"hoped the results would prompt [FSIS] to look into why the drugs are present, what risks they pose, and what can be done to protect the consumer."*

Hundreds of samples of poultry, beef and pork included these drugs. The drug samples were taken from large and small producers. The meat was destined for supermarkets, restaurants, hospitals, schools and elsewhere. FSIS officials have taken no action based on Consumer's conclusions. FSIS insists, the samples were below the thresholds FSIS considers worrisome.

Consumer's food safety scientists disagree. They point out that FSIS cutoffs are greater than other agencies. For example, the FDA has blocked shrimp when it contained levels of Chloramphenicol lower than FSIS standards. The Environmental Protection Agency (EPA) states that FSIS standards are too high. Many European country standards are far below FSIS standards. FSIS doesn't say how FSIS set their standards. It has not advised what the impact of meat within those standards is on human health and life expectancy.

Of course, since they were instrumental in establishing FSIS standards, industry groups stand by the FSIS standards and claim the results amount to fear-mongering. Andrew Gunther, director of A Greener World, a non-profit that promotes sustainable farming, states that *"These are potentially very dangerous drugs, appearing in more samples and at higher levels than I would have suspected."* The source of the drugs could include counterfeit veterinary drugs from India and China that could threaten human health through consumption of food from animals treated with these drugs.

Generally, faster food production processing speeds results in more worker injuries and more contamination of the end food products. Indicative of the trend favoring corporate profits over public safety is a *Washington Post* report that the pork and beef industry will be allowed to increase food processing production speeds, while placing the responsibility for more of the pork and beef processing inspections within their respective industries. The number of federal inspectors will be cut. One of many concerns is giving industry employees responsibility for identifying and removing living diseased hogs when they arrive at the plants before they are processed, supplanting trained FSIS veterinarians. Testing for Salmonella or E. Coli will be reduced or eliminated.

The faster food processing production speeds have not benefitted consumers. A December 29, 2019 *Washington Post* article reported that USDA, thus far for 2019, reported 34 recalls involving 17 million pounds of meat products, a sharp increase from 2009 when there were five recalls involving 1 million pounds. The article reported that, *"Metal parts are breaking off machines that mix, chop and purify ingredients. Plant worker gloves are falling into meat mixes. And bits of plastic and glass from meat packaging and ingredient containers are getting ground into the food."*

A February 19, 2021 Post report indicated that once implemented in a number of processing locations the faster production rates resulted in twice the number of hogs contaminated by fecal and digestive matter when compared to hogs processed in traditional processing plants. These facts were not disclosed to the public though law suits regarding the plants that had implemented the faster production had been filed by Food and Water Watch, the Center for Food Safety and the Humane Farming Association. The Center for Disease Control and Prevention estimates that as many as 500,000 persons become ill each year and 82 die from consuming pathogen laced pork products.

While increased concerns for worker safety are also an issue, FSIS states that worker safety is an issue for the Occupational Safety and Health Administration (OSHA), not FSIS. Thus, FSIS is turning a blind eye towards the very worker safety issues its faster production speeds are creating. This FSIS policy is not unlike the Federal Aviation Agency's deference to the aircraft industry for safety, and in particular for the safety of the Boeing 737 Max airplanes, allowing catastrophic aircraft crashes to occur.

The United States is concerned with terrorism and security, but FSIS ignores a very subtle and lethal means of inflicting harm to large segments of the population of the United States, particularly because much of the food ingredients, drugs and chemicals introduced into the food we eat are produced to in China and India with little or no domestic inspection of those food ingredients. This is an example of a government agency whose primary purpose is to protect the public, but one that is influenced and run by the industry lobbyists, their congressional enablers, and the unknowing voters. Paul D. Thacker, a former staffer with the Senate Finance Committee, led federal investigations into corruption in science and medicine. Thacker, writing for the *Washington Post* stated:

> In July, the American Academy of Pediatrics issued a letter
> that would stop almost any parent in their tracks: chemicals

in food colorings, preservatives and packaging can be dangerous to children, and they aren't being suitably regulated by the
government. A review of almost 4,000 additives found that 64
percent had no research proving they were safe for people to
eat or drink: these chemicals can be harmful to small children
because they are still growing, making them more vulnerable
to any ill effects. The AAP called for reforms to the Food and
Drug Administration food additive regulatory process and
offered guidelines that could be more panic inducing than reas-
suring: don't microwave foods or liquids in plastics, buy fewer
processed foods, switch from plastic to glass or metal whenever
possible, avoid putting plastics in the dishwasher...

Thacker concluded that though the EPA does a terrible job of protecting people from dangerous chemicals, the FDA is worse; both being
closely controlled by the industries they regulate. The same can be said
for ISIS. *The Washington Post* reported that the Center for Disease
Control (CDC) concluded in its annual report that 120 persons died and
25,606 were sickened by food-borne illnesses in 2018 at a healthcare
cost of $3 billion. The article also reported extensively on the conclu-
sions of Eric Olsen, Senior Director of Health and Food, at the National
Resources Defense Council. *The Post* article stated that while,

[better] diagnostic tools may play a role in the [better reporting of food-borne illnesses] lack of appropriate legislation may
contribute to on-going food-borne illness problems such as the
deadly E. coli outbreak in romaine lettuce from Yuma, Ariz.
that sickened 210 people and killed five...was linked to tainted
water in an irrigation canal from a nearby cattle ranch... In
2011, the Food Safety Modernization Act was signed into law...
that required farmers to test irrigation waters which can be contaminated with feces and bacteria. In September 2017 the FDA

suspended those testing and inspection requirements....Recent Increases in the allowable speed at poultry processing plants [are] worrying developments that might herald further upticks in campylobacter and salmonella. They're trying to look at more than one chicken per second to determine if there's a problem. We've delegated a lot of responsibility to the food industry itself. It doesn't always work well....Most experts agree that, despite new technologies and increased attention on supply-side transparency, reports like these highlight our increasingly problematic food system. Food production is becoming more centralized just as food sourcing is going global, so food-borne illnesses have changed and become more dispersed....It is hard to trace the source of a problem when tomatoes come from different farms, say, or leafy greens come from different producers and end up commingled in the same bag.

The Washington Post reported that the Physicians Committee for Responsible Medicine (PCRM), a non-profit group of 12,000 doctors, filed suit against the USDA to prohibit the sale of raw poultry, pork and beef that contain fecal matter. This is allowed by current laws. *The Post* reported that the USDA has a "zero tolerance" for fecal contaminated poultry and meat processing plants. However, this policy only applies if and when the fecal contamination is visible.

A spokesman for the National Chicken Council, a trade group for the poultry industry reported that the USDA has *"a zero policy for fecal matter entering the chiller,"* a large container of cold water and anti-microbial chemicals that chicken carcasses are placed in after slaughter and cleaning. Again, the antimicrobial chemical only controls the growth of bacteria, but allows the presence of fecal matter to remain. *The Post* article reported that the PCRM filed its suit against the USDA after it conducted tests on chicken products purchased from across the nation which made the following findings:

In 2011 the group tested 120 chicken products sold in 15 grocery store chains in 10 U.S. cities for the presence of fecal bacteria. Forty-eight percent of the products tested positive... In April 2012 it tested products purchased in an additional 10 grocery stores around the country; 48 percent tested positive. Then in November 2012, it tested chicken products from 10 grocery stores in Buffalo; 62 percent tested positive. *"Consumers are being misled,"* said Deborah Dubow Press, an attorney for [PCRM], which advocates for preventive medicine through better nutrition. *"We don't like the direction USDA is going, giving the industry more control over meat inspection. They are not doing enough to protect consumers."*

Advocates of too much government are unwilling to deal with shifting the risks of the reduced life expectancy, increased health insurance costs, lost wages and human suffering and deaths that occur when air and water pollution, and food safety standards are reduced to benefit the profitability of large corporations. The reduced life expectancy, increased health insurance costs, lost wages, human suffering and deaths are simply a gigantic unrecognized, tax on the general public.

Who is doing the will of the Father in heaven in today's world? Who are today's Christian heretics?

Chapter 13.

HEALTH CARE

We spend $4 trillion on healthcare in the United States each year. Spending on healthcare dwarfs the bloated military budget. Nevertheless, the United States with less than five-percent of the world's population incurred 25-percent of all Covid-19 infections and 20 percent of all deaths. In 2019 for-profit health insurers returned almost $14 billion to shareholders in dividends and stock buybacks. The healthcare industry is essentially comprised of the pharmaceutical companies, medical device manufacturers, hospitals and medical insurers. Doctors were generally excluded from this discussion. Doctors have generally become employees of health groups and their fees have been largely set or fixed by Medicare and Medicaid.

The Pharmaceutical Industry

Few would quibble with the fact that the pharmaceutical industry provides essential drugs for our health and welfare. A good example is the unprecedented speed with which Covid-19 vaccines were developed, though with billions of dollars in governmental incentives. However, the evidence indicates that drug prices in the United States are generally higher for the same drug than in other countries. Further, persons in the United States pay twice as much for health care as other advanced nations and the United States ranks 31st in longevity among all the nations of the world, and even lower in infant mortality. Further yet, because of the addictive effects and overuse of pain medications causing an epidemic of fatalities, life expectancy in the United States has been declining, even without considering the effects of the Covid-19 pandemic that reduced life expectancy by one year in 2020.

An article by The Center for Public Integrity that was co-authored with the *Associated Press* reported that members of what were referred to as "the Pain Killer Forum," a coalition of drug makers, trade groups and nonprofits had been reporting the vital role prescription pain medications were playing in the lives of millions of Americans. The industry in a report to Congress estimated 100 million Americans suffered from chronic pain, almost half of the adult population; a grossly inflated estimate. Unstated was the fact that the United States accounted for two-thirds of the world's pain medication usage and that many pain medications are addictive.

Also omitted from the report was the fact that deaths from prescription pain killer overdoses of OxyContin, Vicodin and Percocet [opioids] accounted for more fatal overdoses in 2012 than heroin and cocaine combined. Sales of prescription pain killers reached $9.6 billion in 2015. From 2006–2015 the pharmaceutical industry spent more than $740 million on lobbying, including lobbying for opioid-related drug issues. This did not include the millions spent on political campaigns and advertising.

What has begun to happen with opioid addiction and the pharmaceutical industry is similar to what happened with nicotine addiction and the tobacco industry. The harm being inflicted on the general population began causing noticeable harm and death to individuals and increases in state and local budgets for the remediation of pain killer related illnesses, suffering and death. State attorneys generals and local prosecutors began to uncover information and data linking the actions of pharmaceutical industry and distributors with the causes of these increased expenses.

States attorney generals and local prosecutors sued pharmaceutical companies and distributors. The data secured began to confirm that the increased addiction, suffering, illnesses and deaths resulted from the commercial markets being flooded with opioids, and that the pharmaceutical industry was not only complicit, but that the industry lobbied to change laws making it virtually impossible for the Drug Enforcement Administration (DEA) to carry out its mandate to protect the public. A September 16, 2019, *Washington Post* article reported the following facts:

> Newly unsealed documents in a landmark civil case provided clues to one of the most enduring mysteries of the opioid epidemic: How were drug companies able to weaken the federal government's most powerful enforcement weapon at the height of the crises?

> The industry enlisted members of Congress to limit the powers of the DEA. It devised "tactics" to push back against the agency. And it commissioned a "Crises Playbook" to burnish its image and blame the federal government for not doing enough to stop the epidemic.

> The new information is emerging through the efforts of lawyers in the massive federal lawsuit against two dozen drug companies who have obtained depositions from high-ranking company officials, internal company emails and confidential memos. The documents were unsealed in July after a year-long legal fight by

the *Washington Post* and the owner of the *Charleston Gazette-Mail* in West Virginia.

In 2016, the drug companies persuaded Congress and the Obama administration to rein in the DEA and force the agency to treat them as "partners" in efforts to solve the crises. The crowning achievement of the companies was legislation known as the "Marino bill," named after its original sponsor, which curbed the DEA's ability to immediately suspend the operation of drug companies that failed to follow the law.

The full story has never been told because so few of the people involved will talk about it. The list of people who have declined to be interviewed includes former Congressman Tom Marino (R.-Pa.), who first proposed the bill, former acting DEA administrator, Chuck Rosenburg, whose agency surrendered to the pressure, former attorney general, Loretta Lynch, whose department did not stand in the way of the legislation; and finally, then—President Barack Obama, who signed it into law.

The lawsuit, filed on behalf of more than 2,000 cities, towns and counties in federal court in Cleveland, seeks to hold the industry accountable for the opioid epidemic.

The article provides the specific details of the industry's successful efforts to emasculate the DEA, including the names of prominent industry personnel and complicit congressional persons. An October 18, 2019 *Washington Post* article reported the following additional facts:

According to the Center for Disease Control and Prevention, nearly 400,000 people died of drug overdoses involving prescription or illicit opioids from 1999–2017... In July, a [Drug Enforcement Administration (DEA)] database that tracks the path of every pain pill sold in the United States was made public for the first time. The database was released as part of a civil action brought by nearly 2,000 cities, towns and counties... *The Post* found that the volume of pills handled by the drug companies climbed as the epidemic surged, from 8.4 billion in 2006 to 12.6 billion in 2012.

A new report [by the American Society of Actuaries] estimated the epidemic has cost the U.S. economy at least $631 billion and that two-thirds of the toll fell on individuals and the private sector...the epidemic's biggest costs stemmed from the unrealized earnings of those killed by the highly addictive pain killers and health-care expenditures during the four-year study period that ended in 2018. They also projected the 2019 price tag would range from $172 billion to $214 billion... $205 billion... was [attributed] to excess health-care spending for people with opioid-related disorders. Premature mortality costs accounted for $253 billion of the estimated losses, mainly due to the lost lifetime earnings...child and family assistance programs, and lost productivity including absenteeism, lower workforce participation rates and incarceration for drug related crime... $186 billion fell on federal, state and local governments.

Among others, the lawsuits named Purdue Pharmaceutical as defendants. Purdue was largely owned and controlled by members of the Sackler family. Purdue developed OxyContin, a legal narcotic designed to slow the release of the narcotic, oxycodone, to relieve pain and discomfort. Oxycontin was approved by the FDA in 1995. In 2019, the New York Times reported on an audit that showed that for the first 12 years after OxyContin was approved (1995-2007) Purdue's payments to the Sacklers totaled $1.32 billion. In 2007 Purdue pleaded guilty to federal charges that it deceptively marketed OxyContin as non-addictive.

After Purdue pleaded guilty, payments from Purdue to the Sacklers from 2008 through 2017 significantly increased, totaling $10.7 billion. The audit was completed as a part of the bankruptcy filing of Purdue. The Sacklers as a part of a proposed settlement would agree to relinquish ownership of Purdue and pay $3 billion over seven years. They recently agreed to increase this amount. Many of the plaintiffs are questioning the legitimacy of the Purdue to Sackler money transfers. Recipients of the Purdue money transfers included numerous companies, some of which were holding companies controlled by the Sacklers. These companies then transferred to other companies and ultimately to a Japanese division of Mundipharma, a Sackler company that sells opioids and other drugs to foreign markets. Whether these transfers were legitimate remains an open question.

Turning to the issue of "breakthrough drugs," *The Washington Post* reported that in 2012 the Food and Drug Administration (FDA) began to approve so-called breakthrough drugs on a faster than normal approval track based on "preliminary evidence" that they were better than existing treatments. No doubt the faster track significantly reduced the industry's costs of development. The article did not address the costs of the breakthrough drugs being charged to patients, or their effectiveness. However, a Journal of Clinical Oncology study showed there was no evidence they were safer or more effective than the drugs already in use. Further, a Yale School of Medicine study showed that 40% of the approved breakthrough drugs had not been subjected to randomized trials—so much for the FDA's protecting the public, rather than being driven by the dictates of the pharmaceutical industry.

Prescription drug advertising is prohibited around the world. New Zealand and the United States are the only countries that allow prescription drug advertising. In 2015 the American Medical Association (AMA) supported banning consumer advertising for prescription drugs. The AMA also supported measures banning doctors from accepting medical industry payments or gifts intended to influence prescribing habits. The AMA positions made no headway with the executives in the industry or the politicians who received re-election donations from the medical industry and its lobby groups. The use of prescription drugs continues to grow in the United States, while life expectancy declines.

Public Citizen, in Worst Pills, Best Pills News, reported that in November 2020 the Office of Inspector General (OIG) for the Department of Human Service Office issued a "Special Fraud Alert" highlighting the "inherent risks" associated with pharmaceutical and medical device companies paying physicians to speak at company-sponsored events. The Public Citizen report went on to state that:

> Such speaker program events typically involve the physician, who is paid an honorarium, talking about a drug or medical device marketed by the company sponsoring the event. The company often pays remuneration for the attendees in the form of travel expenses, free meals and drinks. The OIG noted that in the last three years, drug and device companies reported shelling out nearly $2 billion to health care professionals for speaker related services.
>
> Companies undoubtedly expect a return on this huge investment. However, getting that return can create an illegal kickback scheme. The OIG referenced numerous OIG and Department of Justice fraud cases brought against companies and physicians involving remuneration paid in connections with these speaker programs that violated federal anti-kickback laws.
>
> Particularly troubling, some of these fraud cases involved drug companies requiring physician speakers to write a minimum

number of prescriptions for the companies' medications as a condition for receiving the speaker honoraria...

A *Washington Post* article, *A Tiny Pharmacy Raises Big Doubts About Drugs*, raised considerable doubt about the FDAs effectiveness in protecting the public from dangerous impurities in drugs, and in drugs that are ineffective and that don't do what they claim they do. Excerpts from the article are quoted below.

> The escalating global recall of Zantac, the heartburn pill that once ranked as the world's best-selling drug, has its roots not in government oversight or a high-profile lawsuit, but in a tiny online pharmacy [in New Haven, Conn.] whose founders feared that U.S. drugs might not be as safe as people think. The pharmacy, Valisure, is a start-up with only 14 full-time employees. But, since its scientists alerted regulators that Zantac and its generic form, rantidine, contained a chemical thought to cause cancer, more than 40 countries from Australia to Vietnam have either stopped sales, launched investigations or otherwise stepped in to protect consumers from possible health risks.
>
> In the United States, the FDA confirmed unacceptable levels of the chemical N-nitrosodimethylamine (NDMA) in some rantidine products—including some syrups taken by babies.

> For Valisure's scientists, finding NDMA was a dramatic example of the kind of discovery they make routinely. Valisure checks the chemical makeup of drugs before it ships them to consumers, and it rejects more than ten percent of the batches for contaminants, medicine that didn't dissolve properly, or pills that contain the wrong dose among other issues. Since late

2018, Valisure has reported more than 50 problems directly to drug companies.

Much of the concern over the quality and safety of the drug supply has been propelled by the massive movement of drug production to foreign factories *"driven by the pharmaceutical industry's desire for cost savings and less stringent environmental regulations,"* [according to Janet Woodcock, director of the FDA's Center for Drug Evaluation and Research]....A 2016 Government Accountability Office (GAO) report found that almost a third of 3,000 foreign drug establishments licensed by the FDA may not have been inspected....The FDA's own data shows that [drug] testing is selective. At the end of 2013 there were 12,100 approved drugs. Over the previous decade, FDA had tested fewer than 4,000... Over the last year, an expanded recall of blood pressure medications have been traced back to a problem in the manufacturing process in factories in China and India according to the FDA. *"We always thought of consumer protection...as an important part of what we would do, but I never appreciated how big of a problem we're watching over... we find more problems than we have resources to fully investigate,"* according to David Light, a partner in Valisure.

Bloomberg Businessweek in its December 16, 2019, issue reported that the FDA can only request manufacturers to order recalls, and that manufacturers can refuse. The FDA has no authority to contact patients directly. Further, though FDA relies on pharmacies, it has no control over how a recall is handled or how effective it is. The FDA has been given authority to order food recalls, vaccine recalls, infant formula recalls and to regulate tobacco products, but bills to grant FDA authority over prescription meds recalls have gone nowhere.

Congresswoman, Rosa Delauro, has attempted to get such legislation enacted. *Bloomberg* reported that the failures to enact legislation were due at least in part to the Pharmaceutical Research and Manufacturers of America; the industry trade group. *Bloomberg* reported that the industry spends $160 annually to make its case to Congress. FDA itself is not asking for the recall authority. Regarding a not yet implemented prescription drug electronic tracking system, *Bloomberg* reported that:

> U.S. manufacturers now create and pass on records of drugs they sell to wholesalers. As of November [2019], both manufacturers and wholesalers are required to put identifying information, including lot numbers, on the labels of products they sell. But wholesalers don't yet have to electronically track the lot numbers of the drugs they sell to pharmacies. The wholesalers have resisted any attempts to require them to do so before 2023. In comments to the FDA in June, a trade group acknowledged product tracing *"will aid enormously in recall administration and effectiveness."* But it said its members couldn't comply without having to enter each lot number—*"a complex string of alphanumeric characters varying in such features as length"* into their data systems by hand, causing *"severe impacts to the delivery needed medicines to patients and healthcare professionals."*

In other words, it's too much work. The legislation exempts pharmacies completely. Even after the law goes into effect, the pharmacies won't have to track which lots they sell to which customers. Nor will they be required to put lot numbers on labels....To further complicate matters, high-volume pharmacies, such as mail-order companies, mix pills from different lots. Pharmacies can also subdivide packages.

✝

Meanwhile, the number of anxious patients mounts. A patient [who had been taking a medication with cancer causing ingredients] learned of a recall from a coworker. He called CVS Pharmacy, which told him he hadn't received the recalled drugs. He contacted his doctor's office but no one had heard of the recall. He took his pill bottle to a friend who worked in a small drug store in a neighboring town. She looked at the bottle, checked online, and discovered the patient's pills were on the recall list.

The Medical Device Industry

Regarding medical devices the industry would like to market as many devices as possible, with as few restrictions as possible, incurring the least cost as possible, to place as many lifesaving and life-improving devices on the market as possible in as short a time as possible. The underlying assumption of the industry's policies are that speed and innovation are enhanced by less regulation resulting in lower costs, greater profits and lifesaving and life-improving devices.

Unfortunately, the number and severity of medical device recalls related to patient harm and deaths indicate that the regulatory balance has swung too far away from protecting the public. The National Center for Health Research (NCHR) reported that the Institute of Medicine (IOM) released a report on the FDA's 510(k) medical device clearance process, a short cut approval procedure, not unlike the fast track pharmaceutical procedure used to review more than 90% of all pharmaceuticals. The IOM report concluded that:

> The current 510(k) process is flawed and should be scrapped. The FDA needs to develop a new system that provides a reasonable assurance of safety and effectiveness. Information that the 510(k) clearance process promotes or hinders innovation does not exist.

NCHR reported that:

> In 2010 an FDA task force recommended numerous changes to strengthen the 510(k) process, but device companies strongly opposed the changes and enlisted numerous members of Congress. As a result, the FDA delayed implementing changes intended to protect public health.

The NCHR stated that the IOM concluded that the 510(k) process can't ensure devices are safe and effective, because FDA bases its approval on the new device's similarities to devices already being used. The IOM concluded that a new system needs to require evidence of and effectiveness to protect the public health. The NCHR also reported that Dr. Diana Zuckerman, president of the National Research Center for Women & Families and the Cancer Prevention and Treatment Fund, stated that *"Too many have been injured or killed by medical devices cleared through this very flawed short-cut known as the 510(k) process... Patients have been harmed by millions of devices including defective hips, heart devices, diagnostic tests and implanted mesh products that haven't been tested on people. All devices that are implanted and life-sustaining should be held to a much higher standard."*

The Washington Post reported that Congress has allowed more time for medical device makers to report to the FDA on medical devices' potential to cause serious injury, including cardiac defibrillators, insulin pumps, breast implants and heart stents. Cardiac defibrillators can run out of battery power during critical procedures. A powerful device designed to laparoscopically remove uterine fibroids spread cancer throughout patients' bodies. A type of breast implant was linked to a rare form of cancer. A duodenoscope had design flaws making it virtually impossible to disinfect. It spread antibiotic resistant infections in patients' bodies.

The Post article reported it may take years for the FDA to detect medical device failure patterns, since it must rely on manufacturers or hospitals to notify it. The FDA and the GAO aren't required to be provided with enough data to estimate the percentage of problems that remain unreported. Doctors who are frequently the first to recognize medical device problems are not required to report incidents to the FDA. One example is Bayer Pharmaceutical's decision to stop marketing its Essure birth control device. Thousands of women reported problems with persistent pain and perforations of the uterus and fallopian tubes, and Bayer has been the subject of more than 16,000 lawsuits by Essure patients. Many complained that the FDA allowed the device to remain on the market far too long in the face of many safety concerns.

The Post article reported that there are approximately 65,000 new adverse events involving medical devices each month. In the 2016 election cycle, medical device manufacturers donated more than $5 million to their favored candidates. They spent $31 million in 2016 on lobbying. The medical device industry's influence is growing, because its user fees fund an ever-increasing percentage of the FDA's budget, rather than the FDA being funded by taxes for the benefit of the public.

The New York Times reported that Dr. Stephen Tower, an orthopedic surgeon had a hip replacement. Five years after the surgery cobalt had leaked from the implant and was destroying local muscle, tendons and ligaments, and even harming the patient's heart and brain. Notwithstanding his attempts to warn his colleagues and Johnson & Johnson, the company continued to market the hip implant. More than 9,000 patients filed suit. About 32 million Americans have a medical device implanted including artificial joints, cardiac stents, surgical mesh, pacemakers, defibrillators, nerve stimulators, eye lenses, heart valves and birth control devices. The quote below has been edited for brevity. *The Times* reported that:

> These devices have helped countless people, and saved lives.
> But many have caused harm—and doctors and patients are at

the mercy of manufacturer's claims about the safety and efficacy of the devices. Medical interventions are now the third leading cause of death in the United States, and devices play an increasing role in that statistic.

Since medical devices didn't come under the control of the FDA until 1976, the agency grandfathered in devices already in use under a provision known as 510(k), which allows manufacturers to sell most new devices without clinical testing as long as the manufacturer says it is "substantially equivalent" or that only "minor changes" were to a previously approved device. The Journal of the American Medical Association found that only five percent of high-risk implanted cardiac devices even partly met the [more rigorous] standard for drug testing.

In 2007 Medtronic recalled the lead wires in its Sprint Fidelis defibrillator after they were found to misfire, harming and even killing patients. The device had not been clinically tested, but the "minor change," thinner lead wires, were more prone to fracture and misfire. By the time of the recall, 268,000 had been implanted. Removal caused its own major complications in 15% of patients.

Even when devices are subject to clinical testing FDA sometimes ignores danger signs. In 1997 during the approval process for a vagus nerve stimulator made by Cybertronics to treat epilepsy, an FDA advisor raised concerns about the high death rate of patients with the device during the trials. FDA granted conditional approval requiring Cybertronics to conduct safety studies after the device was on the market, without warning patients they were being used as unwitting guinea pigs. The FDA approved the studies after it was found FDA hadn't asked for the number of deaths, but only to "characterize" deaths.

With such lax regulations, device recalls have risen. In 2003 there were eight device recalls classified by FDA as indicating a "reasonable probability" that the device will "cause serious adverse health consequences or death." In 2016 there were 117 such recalls affecting hundreds of thousands of patients.

In 1988 President Reagan changed the position of FDA commissioner from civil servant to political appointee, which has meant that presidents, with their war chest fattened by the drug and device industries, have repeatedly appointed industry-friendly commissioners. The FDA is supposed to serve as a bulwark between corporate and the public welfare. It's continued allowance of regulatory loopholes like the 510(k), despite the demonstrated cost to public welfare, calls into question the FDA's fulfillment of its stated mission to protect public health.

The medical device industry lobbying and political donations were effective in having the 2.3% medical device tax imposed by the Affordable Care Act suspended for two years, and now permanently repealed in the 2020 congressional budget agreement. The tax suspension and repeal has the effect of enriching the medical device makers and increasing our deficit. Some would say this is democracy at work. It is not democracy when the wealthy and influential use their undue influence leaving the ill-informed public without a voice.

The Hospital and Insurance Industries

The discussion below generally covers for-profit and nonprofit hospitals. It excludes government hospitals including Veterans Administration hospitals. Unlike for-profits, nonprofits don't pay property taxes and income taxes. Certainly, for-profits must take into account their shareholders' interests which might include minimizing uncompensated care, and low profit or loss inducing activities such as substance abuse and psychiatric services. However, there is little data to substantiate these inherent tendencies and there is little to distinguish differences in the operations between the two.

Health care costs in the United States are double the health care cost in other modern nations. Nevertheless, prior to the Covid-19 pandemic, during the last three years life expectancy in the United States has been declining. The United States ranks 31st in the world in life expectancy, behind much poorer countries such as Costa Rica, Chile, Cyprus, Slovenia, Greece and Malta. The infant mortality in the United States is 25 percent greater than in Canada. *Public Citizen* reported that 100 Americans die every day because of a lack of health coverage. Thirty three- percent reported they stayed away from a doctor, failed to fill a prescription, or skipped a follow-up treatment because they could not afford the expense.

The Washington Post reported that during the pandemic, wealthy hospitals were forced to limit their lucrative elective procedures as a consequence of having to service Covid-19 patients. These hospital groups, through their lobby groups and access to Congress and the administration at the time, were able to secure funding through the Covid-19 bailout legislation that actually made them financially better off than before having to treat Covid-19 patients. In response the CEO of the American Hospital Association replied that each hospital came into the pandemic with its own unique financial situation. Cherry-picking financial data from a few health care systems was not reflective of the struggles facing hospitals in general. It's well known that hospitals serving small towns and rural areas are being forced to close down. Their patients will be forced to seek care at the financially more viable hospitals who lobbied effectively for the more than generous financial funding they received.

Most modern nations have a single payer medical system. The United States' single-payer system is Medicare. However, Medicare generally only provides limited medical coverage for persons 65 years of age or older. Medicare is an efficient system with administrative costs at about 2%, compared to administrative costs of 12% for private insurance. There are considerable private sector impediments to a single-payer system in the United States.

The Washington Post reported that the UnitedHealth Group had $17 billion in profits in 2018; a powerful incentive to maintain the *status quo*. UnitedHealth Group spent $8 million on lobbying. It and other industry groups are resisting the movement towards a single-payer system. American Health Insurance Plans (AHIP), a trade association representing private insurers, and the Healthcare Leadership Council, an industry group including large healthcare providers such as Anthem, have coordinated with Blue Cross Blue Shield, hospital associations and pharmaceutical companies to form the Partnership for American Health Care. The group members spent $143 million in lobbying in 2018, even before the single payer system became a relevant congressional issue.

The September/October 2019 *Public Citizen News* reported that the number of lobbyists working on Medicare for All increased from 29 in the first quarter of 2018 to 270 in the first quarter of 2019, with the overwhelming number *"being employed by hardline opponents of Medicare for All. The vast majority of those entities represent the pharmaceutical industry, hospitals, insurers and other business interests. ... Aside from the increase in lobbying, several coalitions have formed to disseminate misinformation and engage in other opposition activities designed to blunt the momentum of Medicare for All." They were successful.*

The August 26, 2019 *Bloomberg Businessweek* reported that:

> Already powerful interest groups are mobilizing and pooling resources to undermine [Medicare for All] plans. The Partnership for America's Health Care Future—a lobbying group that represents insurance companies, drug makers, hospitals and other industry players—is running TV ads and commissioning polls to undercut support for any expansion of government-provided coverage.

> The industry coalition despises Medicare for All, which would end private insurance, hammer pharmaceutical profits, and slash provider payments as much as 40% in the hope of making coverage universal and accessible.

The Partnership for America's Health Care Future and others are continuing their success in preventing Medicare for All. Who is doing the will of the Father? Who are today's Christian heretics?

Occupational Safety and Health

A 2010 mine explosion in the Massey Energy's, Upper Branch Coal Mine in West Virginia, killed 29 miners. The investigative report found flagrant safety non-compliances with the regulations relating to the ventilation system that allowed explosive concentrations of coal dust and methane to collect and ignite. Massey failed to implement the needed safety requirements, in favor of greater profits. Massey was known for violating safety standards, and was willing to spend money to influence elections. Politicians were fearful of antagonizing Massey, and chose to get re-elected rather than protecting their voters.

The Occupational Safety and Health Administration (OSHA)

activities prevent workplace injuries, disease and death. By limiting OSHA's activities, voters and their elected politicians are in fact
causing increased injuries, disease and deaths of workers. *Public
Citizen* reported that OSHA required certain large businesses in high
risk industries to submit an annual summary of work-related injuries
and illnesses. The rule included anti-retaliation measures prohibiting
employers from discouraging workers from reporting injuries. OSHA
suspended the rule allowing employers to avoid the reports previously
required. This is another example of the government's emphasis in protecting businesses over protecting workers.

Because of congressional budget constraints, OSHA was limited to
2,100 employees who were responsible for the health and safety of
130,000,000 workers at millions of work sites throughout the country;
about 1 OSHA employee for every 62,000 workers.

As an anecdote, the *Associated Press* reported that an excise tax
imposed on coal companies was reduced from $1.10 per ton to $0.50
per ton of underground coal mined because of the congressional inaction. The fund had taken in about $450 million in fiscal year 2017.
The tax was used to fund the Black Lung Disability Fund which paid
benefits and medical expenses of miners diagnosed with black lung
disease. The congressional inaction will cause $15 billion in enhanced
profits for the coal companies at the expense of the public that will now
foot the bill for the miners' expenses.

A March 3, 2021 Washington Post article reported that a Department
of Labor Inspector General (IG) report found that OSHA received more
safety complaints during the 2020 Covid-19 pandemic than during the
same period in 2019 yet performed significantly fewer inspections.
What few inspections were conducted during the pandemic were done
remotely, rather than by on-site inspections, leaving little doubt there
were more accidents, illnesses and deaths. The IG highlighted the fact
that OSHA failed to issue an enforceable standard called an ETS for

coronavirus safety with which workplaces would have been required to comply. This failure resulted from pressure from the administration. Thousands of virus-exposed workers complained to OSHA, but the agency did little to help them. As a result, many workers were sickened or killed.

Certainly, OSHA worker protections add costs to businesses. However, not requiring businesses to pay for their workers' safety shifts the cost of worker injury, incapacity and death to the workers families and the general public. The employers, in most cases large, wealthy corporations, should not be getting a free ride at the public's expense. The public subsidizes and supports increased injuries, disease and death, because the business owners, executives, politicians and voters allow this to happen.

Who is doing the will of the Father in heaven in today's world? Who are today's Christian heretics?

Chapter 14.

MILITARY INTERVENTION AND KILLINGS

We have a new Space Command. We are hearing about a Cyber-Security Command, a hypersonic weapons race and a new strategic nuclear arms race. Certainly, we must maintain military superiority over China and Russia. Because of the military-industrial-congressional complex, spending for military and security related matters will increase to the detriment of education, healthcare and other programs benefitting the public. Domestic terrorism will get a look, but not as much as it should, though it is by far the most immediate and lethal threat to our democracy and way of life. Nuclear submarines and nuclear carrier armadas aren't needed to fight domestic terrorism. There's not much money to be made by the private sector fighting domestic terrorism, so it will languish relatively unattended to, while it becomes an even graver threat, notwithstanding the fact that its dangers, recruitment and lethality have been increasing year after year.

The Constitutional Authority to Declare War

Under Article I, Section 8, of the Constitution, only the Congress has the authority to declare war. Once Congress declares war, under Article II, Section 2 of the Constitution, the President is the Commander-in-Chief of the armed forces. After the attacks by Al Qaeda on September 11, 2001, the Senate by its September 18, 2001, Authorization for Use of Military Force (AUMF), Public Law 107-40, authorized the President to act against Al Qaeda in Afghanistan. The invasion of Iraq in 2003, was authorized by AUMF in Iraq, Public Law 107-243, in October 2002. The latter AUMF was based upon questionable information provided by the administration to the Congress. The invasion of Iraq turned out to be a massive mistake. Al Qaeda in Afghanistan has been defeated and Osama Bin Laden was killed. Saddam Hussein in Iraq has been deposed and killed.

In Afghanistan we are now trying to prop up the Afghanistan government we created against the indigenous Taliban in a country that never had a functioning government that controlled the entire country or one that cared about human or women's rights. These are problems we created by our invasions and our continuing presence there. In Iraq we are again trying to prop up a government we created to keep Iraq from splintering into Kurdish, Sunni and Shia enclaves. We are also trying to keep Iranian influence out and the Islamic Republic at bay. Again, these are problems we created by our invasion and continuing presence there.

Congress has not authorized the continued military actions and killings in Afghanistan or Iraq, or the U.S. military actions in Syria, Yemen, Libya, Somalia and other places. These military interventions are allegedly authorized under the AUMFs, which they clearly are not. They are sometimes rationalized as "not wars", but allowed under the theory that they are Executive Branch prerogatives. The Executive Branch prerogatives have resulted in U.S. military forces being deployed in over 170 countries throughout the world, with undefined missions and unknown expenditures.

These wars and military actions have continued contrary to our nation's best interests, but very much in the interests of military contractors who received $370 billion in 2019. There were 50,000 contractor employees in the Middle East alone in 2019, compared to 35,000 military personnel.

Further, the military has a policy of "collective self-defense." This policy allows the military to attack forces threatening "partner troops" in any of the more than 170 countries, even though this action is not otherwise permitted by law. The very presence of the military actions in foreign lands, and the collective self-defense actions constitute an unlawful expansion of the president's Article II powers. Our tax dollars are supporting these efforts. We are killing and maiming persons and groups we have little or no knowledge of; persons and groups we have never spoken to, let alone negotiated with. Our sons and daughters are involved, and we are financing the killings with our tax dollars.

Many of the killings that result from drone attacks are based on "intelligence" against "targets" that are sometimes nothing more than individuals, groups, clans or tribes cooperating with the United States for a price, but feuding with other individuals, groups, clans or tribes. It has been said that killing by drones can be nothing more strategic than terrorism by joystick. The United Nations' position is that under international law, facilities that contribute economically to a war effort are considered civilian targets. According to a *Washington Post* report, our military air strikes on over 60 sites in Afghanistan alleged to be producing methamphetamine, killed more than 100 civilians.

The Washington Post reported that Yemeni relatives of the victims of a United States drone attack filed suit in the Inter-American Commission on Human Rights for military actions dating back to 2013, when a U.S. drone attack struck a wedding convoy killing several members of the Ameri and Taisy families. The remainder of the killings occurred between 2017 and 2019 from six air strikes that killed as many as 26 Yemeni citizens including 10 children. Witnesses to the raids said that the houses bombed contained farmers, and no militants. Local residents have been traumatized and are daily fearful of additional attacks. Anyone could legitimately ask what the United States is doing in Yemen when no war has been declared, when Congress has probably not even been informed, and the United States has very questionable national interests there. In any event, the Saudis should be taking care of any adverse business on their own borders and in their own back yard.

A purse snatcher can't be arrested without probable cause, or imprisoned without a fair trial. However, a person or group profiting from a U.S. presence can provide "intelligence" about a rival person or group who has no recourse before being killed suddenly, in their own country, thousands of miles away, by a drone attack. Who is doing the will of the Father in heaven in Today's world? Who are today's Christian heretics?

The Christian Just War Theory

St. Augustine commented on the morality of war, and St. Thomas Aquinas provided the outlines of the Just War Theory. Under the Just War Theory, the reasons for going to war must be met, otherwise the killings are murders. Wars for recapturing things taken, or for punishing people who have done wrong, are not justified. Innocent life in the aggressor nation must be in imminent danger and the intervention must be to protect that life.

In 1993 the U.S. Catholic Conference stated that, *"Force maybe used only to correct a grave public evil, for example, aggression or massive violation of the basic human rights of whole populations. Only duly constituted public authorities may wage war."*

Were it not so tragic, the outrage over the 70 fatalities caused by the alleged Sarin chemical bombings in Syria is ironic, when compared to the relative silence exhibited for the more than 400,000 civilian fatalities inflicted by cluster bombs, napalm, barrel bombs packed with shrapnel, phosphorus bombs, artillery, tank munitions and other "acceptable" means of killing. Few, if any, of the numerous non-Congressionally authorized, executive prerogative, military actions being conducted by the United States meet the standards of the Christian, Just War Theory. Certainly, the public should be more aware.

A March 2017 Pentagon investigation revealed 45 civilians killed in air strikes in and around Mosul, Iraq. This investigation omitted another investigation of a March 2017 air strike killing 100 civilians according to residents of Mosul. The Pentagon acknowledged 352 civilian deaths in Iraq and Syria since August 2014, and more than 42,000 engagements in Iraq and Syria from August 2014–March 2017; an average of 43 daily engagements. The 352 civilian deaths plus the 145 deaths in Iraq and Syria do not include civilian deaths from air strikes in Afghanistan, Somalia, Yemen or Libya. In a report to Congress, the military stated it killed 120 civilians during 2018 operations in Iraq, Syria, Afghanistan and Somalia. Outside groups that rely on witness statements and social media put the death tolls at several thousand.

Sarah Knuckey, Associate Clinical Professor of Law, Director, Human Rights Clinic, Human Rights Institute at Colombia Law School, and Alex Moorehead, Director, Project on Human Rights, Counterterrorism and Armed Conflict, Human Rights Institute at Columbia Law School, wrote in the May 31, 2018 *Washington Post* that:

> The government has dramatically increased lethal operations in Yemen and Somalia and according to independent monitors, caused record numbers of civilian casualties in Iraq and Syria...in early May [2018] the White House failed to comply with an... Executive Order requiring it to publicly report on

the number of civilians harmed in U.S. counterterrorism strikes. The government keeps detailed records of the number of civilians it believes it killed in each air strike and raid... For the sake of democratic accountability, Congress should use its oversight powers to ask hard questions of the administration and demand publication of the government's casualty records. Release of these records will help affected civilians, the American Electorate and the international community assess, understand and scrutinize some of the true costs of U.S. military intervention overseas.

Neither the Congress nor the administration is likely to disclose to the public all the killings they are perpetrating in the public's name and with the public's money, contrary to the Constitution, and perhaps contrary to the will of the people, if the people knew the true facts. Too many persons are benefitting and profiting from these actions to fulfill the circle of corruption of getting politicians elected who support these actions.

There is little or no congressional debate about these undeclared wars and killings by the U.S. military thousands of miles away. If there were a debate, it would be predominantly influenced by the military-industrial-congressional complex. Our tax dollars are supporting what could be considered illegal wars and war crime activities. Many businesses, corporations and persons are benefitting from these actions. Politicians are receiving re-election donations for them. Voters are supporting these wars and killings. There should be more awareness and opposition to these actions. Those who hold the sacredness of life at conception dearly should add these issues to their agenda.

The Wisdom of Military Intervention

Leaving aside the fact that there is no constitutional authorization and little or no Christian Just War Theory basis for many of the U.S. military actions, there remains an open question as to whether the United States policy of foreign military intervention is even in our best interests. Had the United States not entered the Korean War, the United States might be dealing peaceably today with a unified Korea that considers China its rival, in the same manner that we are dealing with a unified Vietnam that considers China its rival.

After two decades of warfare in Afghanistan, the U.S. is withdrawing and allowing the Taliban a strong voice in what remains of our propped up government there. As we did with the French in Viet Nam, we ignored history after witnessing that the long years of British and Russian military intervention in Afghanistan resulted in the withdrawal of their forces and cessation of their interventions. Our intervention in Iraq to depose Saddam Hussein has given Iran greater access and influence in Iraq than it ever had there. After Mu'ammar Gaddafi agreed to relinquish his Libyan nuclear program, the United States failed to protect him. He was deposed and murdered in 2011 as a part of the Libyan civil war. Russia is now gaining influence over the United States in Syria, and in what has become a civil war in Libya. It is no wonder that North Korean leader, Kim Jong-Un, is being recalcitrant in committing to denuclearization.

In the Middle East, Mohammed bin Salman, the dictator-king of Saudi Arabia initiated Saudi military intervention in the civil war in Yemen that has resulted in more than a million persons suffering from cholera, tens of thousands of civilians killed by Saudi air strikes, and more than 85,000 children dead from starvation. The Saudis are fighting the war with intelligence, logistic support and weapons purchased under the Arms Export Control Act (AECA); which provides that the weapons received will be used only for internal security and self-defense. It's clear the Saudi actions in Yemen violate the terms and conditions of the AECA, and that little has been done to curtail the Saudi actions.

Our defense contractors are enriched by the fact that Saudi Arabia is spending a portion of its 2018, $69 billion defense budget in the United States. However, the Saudis have been unable to control the Saudi Wahhabi extremist movement that resulted in the Al-Qaeda initiated USS Cole bombing in 2000, the 9/11/2001 disaster, and the Islamic State wars in Iraq and Syria. We've spent much more, year after year since 9/11 to protect ourselves from Wahhabi indoctrinated extremism from Al-Qaeda and the Islamic State than the Saudis spend. The combination of these expenditures creates a huge slush fund providing the undue influence resulting in our unwise policies of continued unwanted and unneeded military presence in the Middle East, while China gains influence and power.

Fareed Zakaria, writing for the Washington Post detailed our lack of foreign policy wisdom and Pentagon waste. Below are a few excerpts:

> Consider two contrasting exercises in power. The United States' F-35 fighter jet program, bedeviled by cost overruns and technical problems, will ultimately cost taxpayers $1.7 trillion. China will spend a comparable amount of money on its Belt and Road initiative, an ambitious set of loans, aid and financing for infrastructure throughout the world, aimed at creating greater inter-dependence with dozens of countries that are important to Beijing. Which is money better spent?

> The Pentagon operates in a realm apart from other government agencies. It spends money on a scale that is almost unimaginable—and the waste is, too. Every government agency is required to audit its accounts, but for decades, the Pentagon simply flouted this law. In 2018, it finally obeyed paying $400 million for 1,200 auditors to examine its books, yet still could not get a clean bill of health. As writer Matt Taibbi noted in a brilliant 2019 expose' of the Pentagon accounting, the auditors

"were unable to pass the Pentagon or flunk it. They could only offer no opinion, explaining the military's empire of hundreds of acronymic accounting silos was too illogical to penetrate." The Defense Department has failed to pass two more audits since then.

Having spent two decades fighting wars in the Middle East without much success, the Pentagon will now revert to its favorite kind of conflict, a cold war with a nuclear power. It can raise endless amounts of money to "outpace" China, even if nuclear deterrence makes it unlikely there will be an actual fighting war in Asia. Of course, there might be budget wars in Washington—but those are the battles that the Pentagon knows how to win!

In 2004, the 9/11 Commission stated that counterterrorism and homeland security must be coupled with a preventive strategy that is as much, or more, political as it is military. We have ignored this policy. After all, there is very little immediate profit in making peace as opposed to war. On September 11, 2018, the Task Force on Extremism in Fragile States, of the United States Institute of Peace (USIP), issued An Interim Report, which concluded, among other matters that:

> Cooperation to prevent extremism is an effective and sustainable strategy that will lower the costs that the United States bears. Already, among the United Nations, the World Bank, the European Union, and the Arab Gulf states, opinions are converging on the importance of tackling extremism in fragile states. If we lead that effort, our partners' resources can leverage our own. Moreover, preventive measures cost far less than military interventions—saving $16 for every $1 invested—and put fewer American lives at risk.

On April 21, 2019, President of the USIP, Nancy Lindborg, hosted a reception at the USIP, with a distinguished panel, and with *Washington*

Post columnist, David Ignatius, as the panel moderator. In Ms. Lindborg's speech leading to the presentation of the Final Report of the Task Force on Extremism in Fragile States, she stated that the Islamic State's influence and support are far greater than al-Qaeda's ever was and that *"We can't kill our way out of this."*

The Final Report concluded that:

> We need a new strategy because costs of our current approach are unsustainable. Over the last 18 years, ten thousand Americans have lost their lives and fifty thousand have been wounded fighting this threat, at an estimated cost of $5.9 trillion to U.S. taxpayers.

Mr. Ignatius, in a later *Washington Post* column commenting on the USIP event, stated:

> We're not talking here about imposing democracy or making the Middle East and Africa look like Switzerland. We're talking the basics—food, water, access to justice, good-enough gover-nance....These mundane anti-fragility tasks don't win medals for soldiers, or get politicians reelected, or make business exec-utives rich, so they end up at the bottom of the pile. Another problem is that this strategy is led by the State Department, the most underutilized and money-starved agency of our govern-ment... We're horrified when bombs ravage places of worship on the other side of the globe. But not enough to do the boring essential thing that has been staring the United States in the face for the last 18 years, which is to slowly help a world that's more just, prosperous and stable.

The United States needs to discontinue its reliance on its volunteer army. The volunteer army frequently draws its recruits from the ranks of those who see the military service as their best or only option. A mandatory lottery draft would spread the recruiting to a more representative segment of the population who would better question the wisdom of our foreign involvements. It's easy to condone military action and misadventures when others are the only ones directly and adversely affected. It has become evident as a result of the January 6, 2021 attack on the U.S. Capital that the volunteer army is contributing to the growth of domestic terrorism.

Who is doing the will of the Father in heaven in today's world? Who are today's Christian heretics?

Chapter 15.

THE ENVIRONMENT: HEALTH AND LONGEVITY

The current rate of technological, economic and social change and their impact on humanity and the earth is unprecedented in human history. We have multinational corporations that can transfer production or even whole industries to foreign lands rendering large geographic areas with under-employment and many poor persons. We have rapid automation and job changes due to technological improvements, robotics and artificial intelligence rendering large segments of the population unqualified for certain jobs, and unable to find meaningful employment. Though business decisions and advances in technology can have adverse localized consequences, they may generally be beneficial in reducing prices and improving the lot of others.

A United Nations report entitled, Intergovernmental Science-Policy Platform on Biodiversity and Ecosystem Services culminated a three-year study by 145 scientists from 50 countries. The chairperson of the report, Robert Watson, a British chemist, concluded that, *"The health of ecosystems on which we and all species depend is deteriorating more rapidly than ever. We are eroding the foundations of our economies, livelihoods, food security, health and quality of life worldwide."* More people require more farm land for crops, more land to live on, more commercial fishing and mining, and more manufacturing and services, which means fewer forests, jungles and natural habitats. One third of the world's land surface and 75% of freshwater resources are devoted to crop or livestock production.

Sea animals are dying grotesquely with stomachs full of plastics. Millions of tons of heavy metals, solvents, toxic sludge and other wastes from industrial facilities are dumped into the world's waters each year. Fertilizers entering coastal ecosystems have created "dead zones" totaling 125,000 square miles. Today there is concern over global warming and climate change due to 37 billion tons of carbon dioxide from fossil fuel burning being released into the atmosphere in 2018 alone. The Earth will likely become uninhabitable in less than a hundred years, among other factors, because of our environmental neglect, according to the deceased, but world renowned astrophysicist, Stephen Hawking.

A report overseen by the United States Global Change Research Program was issued November 23, 2018, with inputs from 13 federal agencies and departments. The report provided an account of the existing effects of global warming, and an alarming account of the accelerating future effects. It is well known that western mountain ranges are retaining much less snow threatening water supplies. Wildfires are destroying ever larger areas during increasingly longer fire seasons. Sea levels are higher. Hurricanes and hurricane caused flooding have become more frequent and more severe. Yield from food supply crops including corn, wheat and soybeans will decrease because of increased growing season temperatures. Cities such as Phoenix will see a doubling of the number of days that temperatures exceed 100 degrees. Financial losses related to labor being unable to work in outside temperatures will total $160 Billion. Coastal property damages could total $120 Billion.

The Economist reported that at one time the north Arctic ice remained the entire year and into the next, reflecting more energy than it absorbed. With the Arctic warming causing permanently frozen ground to unfreeze and expose permafrost and tundra, greenhouse gasses are released. Further, as the organic matter in the permafrost thaws and decays, it releases carbon dioxide and methane. These reactions accelerate the Arctic ice thaw resulting in less energy reflection and more energy absorption creating a perfect storm that is accelerating global warming and climate change. In Alaska and parts of the West the average length of the fire season has increased from 50 days in the 1970s to 125 days in 2017.

The New York Times Magazine reported that Southern California Gas was attempting to plug a methane gas leak in 2015 from an underground cavity in the Alison Canyon Gas field. The leak lasted four months, 25 days longer than the British Petroleum oil spill in the Gulf of Mexico. Approximately 97,100 metric tons of methane escaped, producing the same amount of global warming as 1,735,404 cars in a year. Southern California Gas is currently in bankruptcy seeking to escape the $30 billion in damages resulting from the forest fires associated with its power lines. The suits do not relate to damages caused by the escaping natural gas.

The Washington Post reported that a 2018 methane gas leak from a methane well owned by a subsidiary of ExxonMobil in Ohio leaked at double the rate of the California leak, but was controlled in 20 days rather than four months, nevertheless resulting in 60,000 tons of methane leaking into the atmosphere. Methane is a potent greenhouse gas 25-times as potent and damaging as an equal amount of carbon dioxide. The once permanently frozen ground, permafrost and tundra used to trap methane gas and keep it from escaping into the atmosphere.

Now that permanently frozen ground is thawing at an accelerating rate, methane is bubbling through the once frozen ponds and lakes, escaping into the atmosphere and accelerating the effects of global warming and climate change.

Oil and gas operations leak or vent millions of tons of methane each year; enough to heat 6,000,000 homes. This is a tragic waste of resources. Methane leakage and venting is not regulated. The likes of Southern California Gas and ExxonMobil are allowed to pollute and accelerate global warming and climate change for everyone else without paying the damages that result from their operations. Further, efforts to regulate methane gas leakage are being curtailed as a result of energy business owners and executives, the politicians they control and the voters that voted them into office and allowed them to stay there.

Global warming and climate change have their costs in the higher insurance rates we are now beginning to pay as a result of the more severe and frequent climatological disasters. Further, according to the records of the Congressional Research Service, spending on federal disaster relief remained at about $1 billion in the 1980s. It increased to $4 billion in the 1990s and for fiscal year 2018 was close to $8 billion. These figures do not include disaster relief grants made by the Department of Housing and Urban Development (HUD) or state and local governments.

Because of the undue influence of the affluent landowners and developers, government policies favor rebuilding in previously flooded areas. The Natural Resources Defense Council (NRDC) says that for every $100 the Federal Emergency Management Agency spends to rebuild flooded homes, it spends less than $2 to buyout properties that can prevent recurring flood insurance payments. This policy results in accelerated rebuilding in flood prone areas, with greater public liability.

Indeed, flood prevention measures like the levees constructed along the Mississippi River result in development in the cleared areas that then need additional levees for their protection. The National Flood Insurance Program (NFIP) insures 5 million policy-holders, but renders NFIP liable for $1.3 trillion. The NFIP takes less money in premiums than it pays out to flooded victims annually, but Congress invariably cancels the debt incurred, again, subsidizing the flood risk prone at the expense of everyone else.

The World Health Organization informs that air pollution is the largest environmental health risk contributing to 4.2 million premature deaths per year worldwide. 570,000 children die annually from respiratory infections attributable to air pollution. On a local scale, the town of Waterloo in southern Ontario, Canada, had 19 smog advisory days in 2005. An Ontario Medical Association study estimated that toxic air originating from coal-fired power plants in the Midwestern United States caused 2,000 premature deaths and more than 100,000 cases of respiratory distress in 2005. After Environmental Protection Agency (EPA) regulations limiting coal-fired emissions became effective, air quality improved to the extent that smog advisory days became a rarity in most years.

Under the guise of the Affordable Clean Energy Rule, the EPA began allowing states rather than the federal government to control clean air standards, as if the foul air stayed in the polluting state, contrary to the Ontario, Canada experience. The elimination of federal standards will result in increased asthma, bronchitis, lost wages, increased medical expenses, missed school days, shortened life expectancy and death for the many thousands affected, each year.

The EPA relaxed the requirements for handling toxic coal ash containing mercury, cadmium, arsenic and heavy metals released from our 400 coal burning power plants. These contaminants had been regulated because they had previously spilled into waterways and leached into under-ground water supplies. Regarding the prevention of mercury emissions, a neurotoxin, from coal burning emissions, it costs utilities

$9.6 billion per year versus $6 billion per year in public health benefits. However, the "co-benefits" of reducing mercury also result in soot and nitrogen oxide reductions that result in $37–$90 billion in annual health costs savings and fewer lost workdays, by preventing up to 11,000 premature deaths and 4,700 heart attacks. The EPA sought to eliminate "co-benefits" from its calculations, thus again permitting mercury, cadmium, arsenic and heavy metals to be included in coal burning emissions.

The July 30, 2016 edition of the *Economist* reported that London air pollution has exceeded safe standards by margins so great that breathing London air was the equivalent of smoking for six years, even for infants and children. It's not surprising that *Reuters* reported that a study of more than 50,000 Danish adults aged 50–65 showed that adults living in high pollution areas suffered 17% more heart attacks than adults living in low pollution areas over an 18 year period. Those with a history of heart attacks at the start of the study who were living in a high pollution area were 39% more likely to have a heart attack during the follow up period than those adults living in a low air pollution area.

Persons who vote for politicians that fail to adequately restrict air pollution standards for smokestack and automobile emission are causing the suffering, sicknesses and pre-mature deaths of thousands of people each year in the United States alone. Studies of long-term air pollution show that people living in more polluted areas die prematurely when compared to those living in areas with lower levels of pollution. Fine particles from fuel burning, automobile exhaust, and other sources penetrate the lungs, enter the blood stream and create greater probabilities of heart disease, stroke, lung cancer, asthma and other respiratory illnesses.

The August 29, 2013, edition of *MIT News* reported that air pollution causes 200,000 premature deaths each year in the United States. Each person who dies from air pollution-related causes dies about 10 years earlier than he or she otherwise might have. What should be obvious is that every living human or creature that breaths is also affected, but in less measureable and tangible ways. Our laws properly criminalize the intentional taking of the life of a 93-year-old with a life expectancy of perhaps three years, but allow the 10-year reduced average life expectancy of 200,000 persons, each year. The increased health and life insurance premiums are a giant corporate tax levied on the public by the polluters.

Who is doing the will of the Father in heaven in today's world? Who are today's Christian heretics?

Chapter 16.

THE NATIONAL DEBT: STUDENT DEBT

National Debt

The national debt accumulation rate began to accelerate in the 1980s during the Reagan presidency, because the tax rate reductions enacted then were not offset by spending cuts. The tax rate reductions were implemented in accordance with the supply side economic theory; also known as trickle-down economic theory. Advocates of trickle-down say that reductions in tax rates, especially on the rich who allegedly are the job creators, generate more economic activity that in turn generates more tax revenue offsetting the revenue lost by the tax cuts. The supply-siders disregard the fact that during times when corporations and the wealthy were taxed at much higher rates, there were faster economic growth rates in the gross domestic product (GDP) and less wealth inequality. The GDP is the cumulative value of all goods and services produced within a given time frame, such as a one-year period.

The greater economic activity generated by the reduction in taxes has never been enough to offset the tax revenue lost as a result of the tax cut. The supply side theory is a good example of those with the wealth and influence who benefit from the theory having the political power and influence to accomplish the tax cuts enacted to the detriment of everyone else. David A. Stockman, President Reagan's budget director, confessed that the theory was not workable. President George H.W. Bush called the supply side theory "voodoo economics."

In 2008, the worst financial crises since the 1929 depression was perpetrated by banks and financial institutions disregarding money lending standards and loaning money to unqualified buyers of real estate. Mortgage brokers and banks were incentivized to sell mortgages so that the mortgages could be packaged together as mortgage bonds and sold to investors. Investors and investor advisors didn't know that many of the mortgage borrowers were unqualified and would be unable to make their mortgage payments. Bond rating agencies such as Moody's and Standard and Poor's failed to downgrade the ratings on the mortgage bonds for fear that the banks would take their rating business elsewhere. No one from the rating agencies suffered criminal prosecution or was fired.

Many home buyers defaulted on their loans greatly reducing the value of the mortgage bonds. Faced with losses, financial institutions raised loan standards, thereby reducing the number of qualified buyers. The demand and prices for housing crashed. Banks and other lenders became insolvent or were concerned about insolvency. The government bailed out the banks and financial industry with a massive $700 billion loan, at taxpayer expense. The bailout was shepherded through a compliant Congress, largely as a result of former financial industry executives who then held influential government positions, such as Henry Paulsen, Secretary of the Treasury, formerly with Goldman Sachs. There was no serious consideration of assisting the millions of households that suffered economic hardship as a result of the fraud. No financial industry executives were prosecuted.

According to a report by the Pew Charitable Trusts, the 2008 financial crises resulted in U.S households losing an average of $5,800 in income; U.S households paying an average of $2,050 to mitigate the effects of the crises; U.S households losing an average of $100,000 in stock and housing values; and the stock market losing $7.4 trillion in value.

As a consequence of the 2008 financial crises, the Dodd-Frank Wall Street Reform and Consumer Protection Act was enacted. Dodd-Frank created the Consumer Financial Protection Bureau (CFPB) that crafted rules protecting consumers from fraud from banks, mortgage lenders and credit card companies. The CFPB was funded by fees from the Federal Reserve, not by congressional appropriations. During the period from 2010 to 2016, the CFPB returned more than $12 billion to more than 29 million persons, while imposing $600 million in civil penalties. The idea that an agency was created that looks out for the interests of consumers incentivized members of the Congress to curtail its activities.

Dodd-Frank restricted bonuses to executives making risky investments and required disclosure of how much banking industry CEOs earn versus employee earnings. Dodd-Frank also created the Financial Stability Oversight Council (FSOC) composed of leaders from the Securities and Exchange Commission (SEC) and the Federal Reserve to address risks to the financial system before they damage the economy. Dodd-Frank allowed the FSOC to designate a company as one that is too big to fail if the company's activities posed a danger to the financial system. The law provided that troubled banks whose financial problems become too complicated to solve under the normal bankruptcy process would proceed under the Orderly Liquidation Authority run by the Federal Deposit Insurance Corporation (FDIC). These provisions have been watered down or eliminated.

Besides the significant economic impact and job losses for the general public, the crises also resulted in fewer, but larger, more influential and politically powerful banks and financial institutions, reducing the competition that formerly was of some benefit to the public. Dodd-Frank distinguished between larger investment banks and smaller main street banks. To minimize bank failure risks and to prevent a repeat of the 2008 financial crises, and the $700 billion payout to rescue large banks, the Act precluded the larger investment type banks that also make loans and manage checking and savings accounts, from engaging in hedge fund and private-equity activities.

Bundled loan products of all types remain in great demand. The demand results in the bundling and sale of sub-prime loan products, though not necessarily real estate. Dodd-Frank regulations required banks and financial businesses that constructed and sold bundled loan products to retain at least five-percent of the product they sell. The rationale was that these businesses would have less of an incentive to buy or sell loans of questionable value if they ultimately shared in any losses.

Since the 2008 financial crises, hedge funds, private equity businesses, insurance companies and non-regulated lenders supplanted banks in many lending areas including the bundled loan markets. They purchase and sell the bundled loans rather than making the actual loans. They sued to have the five-percent retention regulation revoked as it applied to them, because they only bundled the loan packages and did not own them. Though the intent of the law and regulations was clear, a court sympathetic to business interests set aside the Dodd-Frank regulation as it applied to these businesses. These unregulated business entities have some unsavory traits, since they can be venues for wealthy and anonymous investors seeking to hide assets, wealth and income.

No good deed goes unpunished. Because of pressure from Congress and the administration, the CFPB was rendered into inactive submission in protecting the public. A CFPB suit against payday lenders was dropped. The lenders had set up operations on Indian Reservations to avoid state lending laws that prohibited deceiving consumers and capping the interest rates that can be charged. An $11 million dollar fine against a predatory lender was also dropped. In another case CFPB lawyers had built a $60 million case against the National Credit Adjusters for illegally impersonating law enforcement officers while collecting debts. The CFPB settled the case for $800 thousand. The size of the CFPB workforce has been reduced and enforcement actions are greatly diminished. These are among the benefits lenders have achieved as pay back for financing the election of politicians more interested in re-election than advocating and promoting the interests of the persons who voted for and elected them.

Since no financial industry executives were criminally prosecuted, the financial industry is still engaging in illegal practices. Wells Fargo, now the country's largest bank, fired 5,300 employees because they failed to meet their quotas in a marketing scheme, involving the opening of over 2 million unwanted savings, checking and credit card accounts customers had not requested. Typically, employees were given a month to persuade customers to open a specified number of new accounts, and gain bonuses, or suffer possible termination if they failed. Many accounts were opened without customer knowledge, exposing customers to identity theft, unwanted credit checks, account fee charges and other expenses. The financial holdings of Wells Fargo's CEO reportedly increased by $200 million during the fraud.

Government borrowing for 2018 was $1.5 trillion; higher than at any time since the 2008-2009 recession. Further, rather than investing the money saved by the tax cuts in development and jobs, corporations and businesses increased stock buy-backs enriching wealthy owners and large shareholders. The 2020 $1.4 trillion spending legislation approved by Congress benefitted the health care industry with $375 billion in tax cuts. Industry patent protection was increased from five to twelve years for "chemically synthesized polypeptide" drugs insuring higher drug prices. Congress failed to limit surprise medical bills from out of network providers or limit the extraordinary increases in prescription drug prices to the inflation index.

The $2.2 trillion Cares Act (March 2020), which was supplemented by the $484 billion Paycheck Protection Program and Health Care Enhancement Act (April 2020) were gigantic, poorly managed laws granting crumbs to the needy and unemployed with gigantic unregulated hand outs to corporate and business interests, hospitals and farmers. Many businesses and corporations offered their workers the opportunity to return to work in unsafe conditions, or lose their unemployment benefits. It's ironic that Chambers of Commerce and big business readily accepted government socialism, while they imposed capitalism on their workers.

The national debt incurred for 2020 alone was $3.1 trillion. The national debt is now almost $28 trillion and increasing rapidly. If it had to be paid off now by the U.S. population of 330,000,000, each person would owe $85,000. Yes that would include welfare recipients, the elderly, the handicapped and children and grandchildren each paying $85,000; a family of four would owe $340,000. The cumulative debt is getting larger each year because as a nation we continue to spend more than the taxes assessed to finance the spending.

The annual interest on the debt, notwithstanding today's low interest rates is about $350 billion, with more being needed to redeem the debt as bonds mature and become due. The debt will preclude spending on needed services for education, research, the elderly and the poor, and for unforeseen emergencies caused by natural disasters or national security dangers. Military and security spending is now politically sacrosanct, because of what the late Senator John McCain called the influence of the military-industrial-congressional complex, expanding on

President Eisenhower's concerns about the military-industrial complex as early as 1961.

We hear much about cutting welfare and imposing more regulations on the needy, but not much about higher corporate taxes, better regulation, and cutting corporate and business welfare to reduce the national debt. We hear much about the need for renovating our failing infrastructure, but primarily by transferring the renovation of roads, bridges, drainage, and flood control to the toll-charging, private sector. Tolls have been as high as $40 for driving a 9-mile segment of Interstate 66 in Arlington, Virginia. One section of the I-395 express lanes in Virginia that had been available free for use in off-peak hours was turned into a toll road forcing off-peak drivers to pay the new tolls, or moving to the regular I-395 lanes, causing traffic congestion where none had been present—more profits for the North American Transurban Group, and more congestion for everyone on non-toll roads.

Unfortunately, especially for our children, grandchildren and most of the rest of us, the tax code revisions palmed off as the Tax Cut and Jobs Act of 2017 was simply more voodoo economics. It benefitted corporations and the wealthy, while increasing the national debt for our children and grandchildren. Among many other benefits granted the wealthy, it reduced the corporate tax rate from 35 percent to 21 percent. The Washington Post reported on a Forbes study showing that as a result the number of billionaires increased by 660 persons in 2020 from 2,095 to 2,755. While the tax cuts were palmed off on the gullible and powerless public as a means to stimulate the economy by hiring more workers, a December 2020 study by the London School of Economics showed that tax cuts consistently benefit the wealthy—and exacerbate the confiscatory concentration of wealth—that results in more undue influence corrupting our democracy.

Who is doing the will of the Father in heaven in today's world? Who are today's Christian heretics?

Student Debt

There are approximately 2.3 million students enrolled in for-profit educational businesses ranging from local trade schools to national on-line universities like the University of Phoenix. Though for-profits are limited to receiving 90 percent of their revenues from government backed loans, military and veteran's educational benefits are excluded from the limitation, rendering the government's liability far greater. Students currently owe $1.6 trillion; more than doubling the $600 billion debt of just ten years ago. The risk for repayment of defaulted loans lies with the general public, not the for-profits. The for-profits get their money up front from the government. The government must then seek recoupment from the students for any loans that are in a default status.

This is simply freeloading at the public expense by for-profit colleges and trade schools, not free-enterprise. Many for-profits provide useful educations resulting in gainful employment. However, some engage in fraudulent, high-pressure recruiting, false promises and inferior educations, leaving their students and graduates with huge debts that can't be repaid.

For example, Corinthian Colleges, Inc. (CCI) had educational outlets in more than 100 locations in Canada and the United States with as many as 77,000 students. The student loan default rate of CCI students and graduates was 19 percent. CCI was investigated for fraudulent practices by Canadian and U.S. officials. CCI closed many of its college locations and filed for bankruptcy. The Department of Education has been chastised by a federal judge for requiring students to continue making loan payments after CCI had been found to engage in fraudulent practices.

ITT Technical Institute had about 130 campuses in 38 states. ITT was accused of high-pressure recruiting, high rates of student loan defaults, and poor educational standards. The U.S. Dept. of Education prevented students from using the student loan program to attend ITT colleges. ITT closed its campuses and filed for bankruptcy.

DeVry University was charged by the Federal Trade Commission with misleading applicants by claiming that 90% of its graduates landed jobs in their fields within six months after graduating, and that bachelor's degree graduates of DeVry averaged 15% higher incomes than other colleges. DeVry settled the claims against it by agreeing to a $100 million settlement with the FTC. In his book entitled *Tailspin*, Steven Brill reported that the Education Secretary, Betsey DeVos hired a former DeVry University Dean to head the unit responsible for investigating fraud. For Steven Brill the for-profit education issue is only one of many examples of the corrupting effect of money in politics. Even Jerry Falwell Jr.'s Liberty University, reported its loan repayment rate was "poor" when compared to an undefined national average.

Federal regulations had required for-profit educational businesses to inform student-applicants about their previous graduates' ability to find gainful employment and make loan payments. For-profits were also required to meet minimum educational standards to qualify to engage in the government financed student loan program. Further, to protect the public interest, regulations limited the amount of debt students could incur. The Department of Education changed or eliminated the regulations intended to protect applicants for admission, students and the public. The general public ends up financing the profits of the for-profit businesses masquerading as educational institutions.

To make matters worse a report by the Education Department's, Inspector General advised that the Department imposed barriers, and reduced the staff that processes student loan applicants seeking forgiveness of their debts based on fraud. Not reported by the Inspector General was the fact that the regulations limiting the amount of debt students could incur were revoked. To make student financial matters worse, it was reported that the Consumer Financial Protection Bureau suppressed a report that the nation's largest banks were defrauding students by imposing improper account fees. The general public subsidizes defaulted loans that increase the wealth of the owners of unscrupulous for-profit colleges and universities, as assisted by the hierarchy of the Department of Education. Hopefully, these actions against students and the general public will be rolled back

Who is doing the will of the Father in heaven in today's world? Who are today's Christian heretics?

Chapter 17.

PRISON REFORM

"I was in prison and you visited me...And when was it when we saw you sick or visited you in prison?...Truly I tell you, just as you did to one of the least of these who are members of my family, you did it to me" (Matthew 25:36-40). "Remember those who are in prison as though you were in prison with them" (Hebrews 13:3). "Let the groans of the prisoners come before you; according to your great power preserve those who are doomed to die" (Psalm 79:11).

Our Two Million Incarcerated Citizens

The tough-on-crime policies that criminalize minor drug offenses and impose mandatory sentences, including life-sentences for three felonies, have contributed to the more than 2,000,000 persons imprisoned in the United States. This is 500,000 more prisoners than China, which has five times our population. Persons are imprisoned for five years for non-violent offenses such as being in possession of five grams of a prohibited drug. This incarceration policy is to be contrasted with the blind spot provided to the executives of the tobacco, banking and finance industries who suffered no prosecutions or convictions for the deaths, suffering, medical expenses and hardships they perpetrated by their fraud. The imprisonment policies became law largely as a result of the lobbying and influence of the corrections industry under the guise of protecting the public.

At least 37 states have legalized the contracting out of prison laborers in privately run prisons to work for corporations for little or no pay. Though Amendment XIII to the Constitution abolished slavery, the Amendment hasn't been made to apply to persons convicted of crimes. Laws that protect workers such as minimum wage or even workmen's compensation that compensate workers for work related injuries or death have not been made to apply. Prison officials preclude incarcerated persons from forming unions and many even preclude prisoners from petitioning for redress. Many prisoners leave prison in poverty which greatly contributes to recidivism.

The Lockhart Prison in Texas manufactured air conditioning parts for Henderson Controls, Inc., and computer boards for OnShore Resources. Prisoners were paid from $7.78 to $10.28 per hour. However, deductions were made for taxes, room and board, dependent support, restitution, and to a crime victims' fund. The prison advertised that $20 million was returned to the state since 1993. Lockhart did not report how much the prisoners were left with, if anything, after the deductions, or how much Lockhart was paid by Henderson and OnShore for Lockhart's prisoner labor. Prison labor dates back to 1849 in Texas; before the civil war, to cotton and wool textile plants. Prison labor had its roots in slavery, and at least in Texas, not much has changed.

In terms of the efficiency of running a private prison, the privately-run prison in Lawrenceville, Virginia, reportedly had only five guards for 750 prisoners during the day and only two at night. For any infraction by a prisoner, 30 days can be added to the sentence, or good behavior time is lost, thus insuring longer prison terms and greater profits for the privately-run prison. Privately-run prison inmates are eight times more likely to have their incarceration time increased than in state run prisons.

Prisoners in certain state prisons are frequently forced to pay $1.50 per minute for telephone calls that cost less than $0.03 per minute on a commercial phone card. The prison phone service companies benefitting from these exorbitant rates shared $460 million dollars with the states allowing the companies' monopolistic prison phone services. The fact that prisoners and their families cannot stay in touch and the effects on recidivism are apparently irrelevant.

At least for now Securus Technologies plans to buy Inmate Calling Solutions have been curtailed. The proposed merger would have resulted in 90 percent control of prison inmate telephone usage. Nevertheless, since states are benefitting from these monopolistic practices in the form of paybacks, it is unlikely that any progress will be made in reducing prison phone rates to reasonable levels. These practices against an incarcerated and helpless population are being perpetrated by the owners and executives of the industries profiting from these practices, the politicians beholden to them, and the voters who voted them into office.

Cruel and Unusual Punishment

Constitution Amendment VIII prohibits the infliction of cruel and unusual punishment. As of 2008, more than 80,000 incarcerated persons were in solitary confinement. The practice has become common-place with the increased privatization and management of prisons. Prisoners are often confined for months or even years in solitary confinement. There is no federal or state reporting system that tracks prisoners in solitary.

The American Friends Service Committee of the Quaker Church reported that solitary confinement included severely limited contact with other humans in confined and dark quarters for 22–24 hours per day for extended periods. Visitation for prisoners in solitary can be limited and inadequate medical and health treatments can result. Restricted reading and personal property can be imposed. Physical torture such as being hog tied, or confinement to restraint chairs, or loud noises can be imposed. Sensory deprivation, permanent brightness or darkness, extreme temperatures and forced insomnia can be imposed. Stun guns and grenades can be used as torture, along with other forms of brutality.

The conditions described as being imposed have resulted in visual and auditory hallucinations, hyper-sensitivity to noise or touch, insomnia and paranoia, uncontrollable rage and fear, distortions of time, increased risk of suicide and Post Traumatic Stress Disorder. The prison isolation described fits the U.N. Convention Against Torture which defines torture as any state-sanctioned act, by which severe pain or suffering, physical or mental, is intentionally inflicted for information, punishment, intimidation, or for discriminatory reasons.

Prisoners are placed in solitary confinement for a variety of reasons from serious infractions such as violence against other inmates to minor offenses such as talking back to a guard or being in possession of a cell phone or cigarettes. Solitary confinement is used for talking to a suspected gang member. However, it is also used as retribution for forms of activism including better prison conditions such as better protection against abuse and better library and health services.

From an international perspective government officials escaped official sanctions and criminal prosecution for allowing the use of dogs to frighten prisoners being interrogated and authorizing prisoners to be hidden to avoid being registered with the International Committee of the Red Cross. These are clear violations of Army regulations and the Geneva Conventions. Amnesty International reports that were critical of conditions in Iraq and Cuba were cited by the same top government officials as reasons to take official action including military attack. However, when Amnesty International called the U.S. prison in Guantanamo Bay, Cuba the Gulag of our times, top government officials called the report absurd.

Excessive Bail and Fines

Defendants who are awaiting trial, even for traffic cases, frequently remain in jail if they're too poor and destitute to post bail. If they're too poor to post bail, and are languishing in jail, they can't work so they become even more poor and destitute, and are forced to be away from their families and children. Amendment VIII to the Constitution provides that:

> Excessive bail shall not be required, nor excessive fines imposed, nor cruel and unusual punishment inflicted.

Defendants too poor to post their own bail, but not totally destitute, resort to bail bond companies to post bail and receive limited freedom until trial. Judge Joseph A. Migliozzi and Heather Long wrote in an article for the August 2019 Virginia Lawyer that the Prison Policy Initiative found that over the past 15 years, pre-trial detainees account for 99% of the jail population growth. Six out of ten people incarcerated in the United States are awaiting trial. That is almost half a million people on any given day; 465,000 people nationwide in 2018.

California and other states began to enacted legislation to help mitigate the prejudice of exorbitant or unreasonable bail fees against the poor. The legislation generally leaves the issue of bail up to the courts, allowing the courts to decide to release, or have the charged person remain in custody based on a number of factors, including the nature of the charge, the defendant's record, and the defendant's ties to the community.

Bail bond companies are not in favor of the legislation, because it will likely have a negative impact on their bail bond business. In California the bail bond industry raised millions of dollars to have such legislation repealed. Without a steady stream of bail bond applicants, the investors who loan money to the bail bond companies would find other places to invest.

A related problem are state laws requiring the automatic suspension of drivers licenses for being unable to pay fines and costs assessed by courts for traffic offenses and criminal convictions. Local jails were sometimes full of persons incarcerated for these reasons. Angela Cioffi, Executive Director of the Legal Aid Justice Center, writing for the Virginia Lawyer, noted that such laws are punitive, counter-productive and likely unconstitutional. After five years of a pro bono effort, a local law firm achieved a temporary suspension of the practice bringing relief to nearly a million persons in Virginia alone.

Constitutional Amendment VIII prohibits excessive fines. Constitutional Amendment XIV prohibits states from making or enforcing any law depriving citizens of life, liberty or property without due process of law. Indiana's seizure of a vehicle worth $42,000 for a $200 drug transaction would appear to be an excessive fine. However, such a disparity is not unusual under state civil forfeiture laws that are used to engage in a lucrative form of law enforcement.

An Indiana trial court ruled that such a taking was grossly disproportionate with the crime. However, the Indiana Supreme court, deluged with petitions from chambers of commerce and municipalities complaining they would lose revenue, overruled the trial court. The Indiana Supreme Court ruled that it was questionable that Amendment XIV, ratified in 1868, in fact made Amendment VIII, ratified in 1791, applicable to states. Fortunately, the Indiana Supreme Court was overruled by the U.S. Supreme Court.

Who is doing the will of the Father in heaven in today's world? Who are today's Christian heretics?

Chapter 18.

GENETIC RESEARCH

G enetic research is currently regulated on a country by country basis. Meaningful international attempts to regulate genetic research are unlikely to yield results. There is little leadership in the United States for such an effort, and the United States' track record on international agreements has not been good. The United States has declined to be bound by the International Criminal Court, the Mine Ban Treaty, and withdrew from the United Nations Framework Convention on Climate Change, and the Joint Comprehensive Plan of Action to control Iran's nuclear program, though Iran was in full compliance with the agreement. The United States' has proved itself to be an unreliable partner when it comes to international agreements, and there is little or no leadership incentive for a treaty encompassing genetic research.

It was widely reported that a genetic scientist in China announced he had created embryos from couples with an HIV infected father. The scientist then edited the embryos' DNA to disable the gene that allowed the HIV to infect cells. The scientist's position was that it was proper to use gene therapy for healing, but not to engage in gene therapy to achieve designer-type babies with enhanced IQs or selected hair or eye coloring.

Other scientists were critical stating that there are other safe and effective ways to protect children from HIV transmission. Thus, there was no unmet medical need. Other scientists were critical because if the altered embryos were implanted, were born and became adults, they could transmit their altered genes in perpetuity permanently altering the human race. Further, any detrimental effects on humans with the altered genes and their offspring were unknown at the time. The scientist's work was allegedly conducted off campus with the employing university being unaware of the work.

The Washington Post reported that researchers had been able to alter the MYBPC3 gene in an embryo. This gene causes a disease of the heart muscles, but with no symptoms. It remains undetected, unlike the gene allowing the transmission of HIV. Inheritors of the gene will suffer a sudden cardiac death. There is no known method to prevent or cure the problem. One in every 500 persons is allegedly affected by the disease worldwide, primarily in India.

The research involved eggs from 12 female egg donors and sperm from a male who carried a defective MYBPC3 gene. After the defective sperm was injected into the healthy eggs, the embryos were allowed to grow for a few days. There was no plan to implant them to create a pregnancy. The problem gene was then removed using the "CRISPR" method which allows gene removal at the molecular level. Once the gene was removed, the non-mutated copy of the gene from the healthy female egg donors' genes took over. Seventy-two percent of the defective genes in the embryos were corrected.

Once the results of the experiment became known, the embryos were terminated. In the case of the MYBPC3 gene, there is no known post birth cure. If the embryos without the problem gene had been implanted causing a female to become pregnant, a child without the defective gene would presumably have been born. The gene snipping did not result in any known changes in the related or adjacent DNA; at least none were detected at the time. Off target changes can result in future adverse side effects. If the diseased DNA extraction were to be used on all known MYBPC3 carriers, the disease could be eliminated through natural evolution.

The experimentation with the MYPBC3 gene was apparently proper since there was an unmet medical need, but improper because it could have altered the human race by eliminating a gene that could cause sudden death in adults if implanted with the intention of creating a pregnancy. Another objection by those who claim life begins at conception would have prohibited the use of embryos in any experiments. These were privately funded experiments.

The article stated that, *"The United States forbids the use of federal funds for embryo research, and the Food and Drug Administration is prohibited from considering any clinical trials involving genetic modifications that can be inherited. A report from the National Academy of Sciences, Engineering and Medicine... laid out conditions by which research should continue. The new study abides by those recommendations."*

In other procedures disease generating DNA was extracted from DNA controlling women's appearance and other major traits. The altered DNA was then inserted into a healthy donor egg and fertilized with the sperm of the husband of the woman whose egg would have produced a diseased infant. The same type of procedure could be used to inject the DNA of older women into the eggs of younger women allowing older women to be able to bear their own genetic children.

In 2015 Congress prohibited genetic editing of inheritable traits, and the exportation of the results of such editing. The procedure is not prohibited in other countries including Britain and China. Some ethicists fear that these techniques can enhance human traits beyond simply eradicating a disease. The National Academy of Sciences does not allow genome editing for purposes other than treatment or prevention of diseases or disabilities. However, enhancing certain traits such as eyesight for persons likely to inherit vision problems or color blindness, or changing the height for persons likely to be in the lower 10th of the human height percentile, or the highest 90th of the human height percentile could improve the quality of life for many.

Genetic experiments with embryos and fetal tissue present problems for those who believe that life begins at conception. Restrictions on the use of embryos and fetal tissue research are being implemented and proposed. Researchers have bred mice with weakened immune systems that have been injected with immune system tissue from aborted fetuses. These altered mice essentially develop a human immune system of fundamental value for biomedical research. These experiments and research are likely to be restricted

Research in Sweden using fetal cells was instrumental in the development of the polio vaccine. Research using fetal tissue has been instrumental in developing therapies for HIV, various cancers, sickle cell anemia and other diseases and conditions. If research involving fetal tissue is prohibited in the United States, vaccines and treatments for Covid-19 and other diseases are likely to come from other countries. Would these remedies be allowed in the United States, or would persons desiring to avail themselves of these remedies, and who could afford the cost, have to travel to another country? Would the adverse scientific and economic impacts of prohibiting research using fetal tissue in the United States be acceptable?

An Ohio cryogenic storage facility for human female eggs and embryos had a power failure that destroyed the 4,000 stored eggs and embryos. Many persons whose eggs and embryos were stored were justifiably upset and angry that their future, potential children had been destroyed. Some were suing to hold the storage facility operators culpable for murder. It's interesting that these persons would consider their artificially created embryos, stored outside the womb, in a cryogenic facility at minus 320 degrees Fahrenheit, to be alive and with a soul, when no human could survive under those circumstances.

Those who believe life begins at conception are to be commended for the sacredness with which they hold human life. Certainly, their personal beliefs, religious beliefs and human rights should never be encroached upon or violated. Their activism for the sacredness of life and their efforts to preserve the life of an embryo would be most welcome for the sacredness of lives lost because of inadequate gun control; the sacredness of the lives lost due to capital punishment; the sacredness of lives lost due to inadequate air and water pollution regulations; the sacredness of lives lost due to inadequate food safety standards; the sacredness of lives lost due to inadequate coal mine and worker safety standards; and the sacredness of the lives lost because of our endless wars and the profits being derived from them. Most fertilized human female eggs never implant in the womb, and are excreted during female menstrual cycles. It is unknown whether those who believe life begins at conception would make an exception for souls excreted during female menstrual cycles.

We give infants shots to eliminate communicable diseases such as measles. We then complain when everyone doesn't get the measles shot, and measles is reintroduced into the human population, after it was thought to have been eradicated. Infants are vaccinated against non-communicable diseases such as polio. Ebola is very communicable and frequently fatal. It reappears in the Congo on a regular basis and has spread to the United States. The flu virus alters itself on a regular basis and inflicts annual suffering and death. The jury is still out on whether the Covid-19 variations and permutations can be fully controlled through vaccinations. If genes can be altered to make humans more resistant to these diseases, irrespective of their communicability, and humans are cured of them in perpetuity, then perhaps human genes should be altered.

Today under the theories of capitalism and the freedom to pursue entrepreneurial endeavors we allow genetically modified animal growth hormones to accelerate growth for purposes marketing and slaughter. We use modified animal feeds and antibiotics to improve animal survivability and accelerate growth rates. We modify plant seeds to resist drought, disease and insects. Today, we allow post-birth facial plastic and bodily surgery, breast implant surgery, make up, hair coloring, tattoos, tooth implants, teeth whitening, colored contact lenses, liposuction, stomach surgery for weight loss, intra-uterine fetal surgery, and medication to accelerate human growth. These are now commonplace procedures. It begins to be difficult in deciding the ethics or morality of changing or affecting pre-birth traits, while allowing similar traits to be altered at will after birth.

Who is doing the will of the Father in heaven in today's world? Who are today's Christian heretics?

Chapter 19

GUN SAFETY

In the 10-year period between 2005 and 2015, there were 71 deaths attributable to terrorism in the United States. During the same 10-year period there were 301,797 deaths attributable to gun violence, an average of 82 persons killed every day. Two children under the age of 18 are killed on the average every day due to gun violence. A toddler shoots someone with a gun on the average of once a week. If a mass shooting is defined as an incident where four or more persons were shot, then mass shootings occurred in more than 100 metropolitan areas in the United States in one year.

High school and college aged children in the United States are 50 times more likely to die by being shot than their peers in other advanced countries. In the United States alone, children younger than 15 accounted for 91% of all the gun deaths in all advanced countries. In 2016 more than 150,000 persons were killed or wounded in the United States by guns. The annual cost of gun violence is estimated at $200 billion.

New Jersey senator, and presidential candidate, Cory Booker, claimed more people have been killed during his lifetime [since 1968], than in all the wars the United States has been involved in. Data shows that there have been about 1.4 million deaths attributable to all the wars since the Revolutionary War. The fact that Cory Booker can make such a colorable claim regarding the last 51 years is indicative that gun violence is a serious social problem with a significant economic impact.

We have the Transportation Safety Administration (TSA) intrusively inspecting airline passengers and their baggage to control deaths from terrorism. We have U.S Marshalls on virtually every airline flight. We have the CIA and the FBI actively monitoring, conducting surveillance, investigating and prosecuting alleged terrorism suspects. We have banks and retail establishment monitoring and reporting significant cash transactions to identify terrorism suspects. The total expenditure for anti-terrorism is unknown but no doubt totals many billions of dollars.

The effort to combat terrorism to save lives needs to be contrasted with the effort to save lives from gun violence, where any bigoted, deranged, paranoid or mentally unstable person, anyone with a grudge, a disgruntled employee, or a perpetrator of domestic violence can buy automatic weapons and murder scores of innocent persons with impunity.

The technology for safer guns and better background checks exists, but little is being enacted or implemented. The Gun Control Act of 1968 prohibited gun possession by mentally defective persons. Federal regulations established a rule requiring the Social Security Administration to identify and submit the names of the 75,000 beneficiaries, annually, that require a representative to manage their benefits, to the gun background check system. Regulations also required the beneficiaries to be notified and allowed them to appeal the determination.

Congress rescinded the rule. This simple but effective regulation was abolished because of the owners and executives in the affected firearm industries, the politicians beholden to them and the voters who voted for them. Twenty-three thousand doctors and health professionals who treat gun violence almost daily signed a letter urging research on gun violence. The National Rifle Association (NRA) told them essentially to "stay in their own lane."

The fact that the United States has the most lax gun regulations of all modern nations and the highest murder rate hasn't deterred the NRA political and propaganda machine from calling for still more guns. This is an example of the very well organized financial and political clout furthering the interests of gun and ammunition businesses to the detriment of the general public.

CHAPTER 20.

SCIENCE AND THE UNAFFILIATED

Here on this fleck of a relatively insignificant Earth, one has to be awed by the indescribable beauty of Yosemite, the Grand Canyon, Crater Lake and other natural wonders; by the sight of a magnificent 2,500-year-old California Sequoia that stands as high as a 25-story building; by astrophysicists studying light, radiation and neutrino particles just arriving at the Earth that originated from events that occurred hundreds of millions of years ago; by the beauty, complexity and practical effects of Einstein's theory of relativity; by quantum mechanics, the study of the forces, waves and particles of sub-atomic matter; the uncertainty principle; and the string theory that seeks to consolidate the laws of the cosmos with the laws of quantum mechanics.

In this lifetime we'll probably never have scientific proof that God exists. Dean H. Hamer, a behavioral geneticist at the National Institute of Health claims to have discovered the god gene; a gene known as VMAT2. He equates spirituality with the feeling of transcendence. He found that certain brain chemicals including serotonin, dopamine and norepinephrine appeared to be in play during the deep meditative states of Zen practitioners, Roman Catholic nuns and the mystical trances induced by mind-altering drugs. The VMAT2 gene regulates the emission of these substances. These substances are thought to play a major part in regulating brain activities associated with mystic beliefs.

Critics in the scientific community say Hamer's conclusions are simplistic and speculative, because his findings rely too much on anecdotal evidence and not enough on testing the VMAT2 gene to determine other possible links to certain behaviors. The VMAT2 gene allegedly accounts for less than one percent of the variance in transcendence scores. Critics doubt that Hamer's findings can be replicated, which is necessary as a basis for scientific proof. In any event, Hamer's research does not answer the question of whether there is a god, and why some persons believe in the existence of a god, and others do not.

How does the existence of deities relate to all this? Yes, deities. God did not banish Adam and Eve from the Garden of Eden because they ate from the Tree of Knowledge. God banished Adam and Eve because of God's concern that Adam and Eve would eat from the Tree of Life, and become immortal like the gods (Genesis 3:22-24). If we don't destroy ourselves first, perhaps our scientific knowledge will eventually allow us to eat from the Tree of Life and become immortal like the gods. Would atheists still be atheists? Or would religion disappear?

World renowned astrophysicist, Stephen Hawking, now deceased, believed that science and evolution can explain our present-day world without God. Albert Einstein believed in a god of the cosmos, but not one that cared much about human behavior or salvation. Atheists insist that a god based on a human need or hope, or on an ancient writing provides no basis at all for the existence of God. Many atheists write convincingly, questioning or debunking the existence of a god. Though atheists might be correct, let us first consider what we don't yet know.

Though extraordinary, the Hubble spacecraft-telescope sees only the visible light frequencies from the electromagnetic spectrum. Cosmic dust blocks the light emitted from the oldest parts of the universe impeding Hubble's ability to see these parts. Light travels almost 6 trillion miles in just one year; a light-year.

To gain some perspective about the immense distance that light travels in a year, one light-year would be the equivalent of about 32,000 round trips from the Earth to the sun in a year; that would be 88 round trips each day. If a solar storm created radiation that could disrupt communication systems on Earth, the light from the storm and the Gamma radiation would take only about 8 minutes and 33 seconds to travel the 93,000,000 miles from the sun to the Earth.

To gain some perspective of the immensity of our universe, the nearest stars to our sun are Alpha Centauri A and B, that revolve around each other. They are about 4.2 light-years away. They are in the Milky Way Galaxy in which our Earth and solar system are located. The nearest galaxy to the Milky Way Galaxy is the Andromeda Galaxy which is 2 million light-years away. Recently, a collision between two neutron stars occurred that was 200 million light-years from the earth.

Neutron stars are so dense that a tablespoon would weigh several billion tons. To gain some perspective of the neutron star density, a tablespoon of concrete would weigh about two ounces. A neutron star collision occurred 130 million year ago, but the light and other radiation is just arriving here at our earth. Because of the immense density of neutron stars, in addition to electromagnetic radiation such as light, X-Rays and Gamma-Rays, the collision generated newly discovered gravitational waves that were predicted by Albert Einstein.

Jeffrey Kluger writing for *Time* reported that NASA is in the midst of developing the Webb telescope-spacecraft that will analyze the infrared frequencies of the electromagnetic spectrum, allowing Webb to peer back 13.6 billion years, only 200,000 million years after the so-called big bang occurred. The infrared frequencies also travel at the velocity of light. The vastness of the universe can somewhat be grasped by realizing that we will be seeing our universe through the infrared spectrum, traveling at the speed of light, not as it presently exists, but how it existed 13.6 billion years ago.

Webb will allow us the possibility of seeing the formation of the first galaxies or the first planetary systems. What we'd be seeing would not be what currently exists, but what existed 13.6 billion years ago in a cosmic Netflix or Amazon type of streaming process. X-Ray telescope-spacecrafts and others are in the conceptual design phase. They could allow humans to study black holes or analyze the atmosphere of planets to determine the existence of methane and carbon dioxide which are associated with life. Of course, that would only be life based on the carbon supported system of life as we know it, not life as it might otherwise exist. After all, the planet Saturn has diamonds as rain rather than the water rain here on earth.

Unfortunately, the Webb telescope-spacecraft has been plagued by continuous technical problems, delays and overruns. The current estimate for its launch is October 2021.

Though the big bang theory is considered the beginning of time and space, it is not the beginning. There was matter, space, energy, and time before the big bang that contracted into an infinitely small space, creating an infinitely large density that resulted in the cosmic chemical and physical reactions we conveniently refer to as the big bang, eventually evolving into the formation of the galaxies, our sun and solar system including planet Earth. There may have been similar events in other parts of space at different times. This big bang might not have been the first. Could there be an omniscient entity or entities from a parallel or previous universe controlling our present universe? Could this omniscient entity be our God?

We wonder about life on other planets, the mystery of black holes, the possibility of parallel universes, and the enormous volumes of undetectable matter in our universe. Life here on earth began developing 3.7 billion years ago. We humans as homo-sapiens developed just 300,000 years ago, displacing or perhaps incorporating the genetics from our Neanderthal cousins. Perhaps life elsewhere existed and became extinct as it may become extinct on this Earth. Or perhaps life elsewhere existed and became all knowing, omniscient and all powerful.

In quantum mechanics matter and energy possesses particle and wave properties that can be in many places at the same time, perhaps not unlike the dark energy and dark matter discussed below. The quantum mechanics waves are not the same as the electromagnetic spectrum waves. The quantum mechanics waves can somewhat be described in terms of the probability of where and how often the particle aspect of the waves is likely to be. It is not known if the waves have real substance, or if the probabilities are simply a calculating tool to determine something about the wave function. The range of places the matter can be found follows a statistical pattern as the function of a wave equation.

When a measurement attempt is made to determine where the quantum matter is at any given moment, the location of the particle aspect of the matter can be found, but the wave function ceases to exist. Thus, though the matter can be located within a degree of probability, it is not the same matter that was originally sought to be measured. The observers-measurers produce the results of the measurement and affect the result. The question arises as to whether the wave function is a part of reality, or a descriptive tool. Eugene Wigner, a 1963 Nobel Prize winner for physics, suggests that it is the consciousness that brings reality into being.

We learned above that neutron stars are so dense that a tablespoon would weigh several billion tons, and that by comparison a tablespoon of concrete would weigh about two ounces. Karl Schwarzschild, a German scientist, used Einstein's equations to conclude that if matter approached an infinite density, for example, more dense than a neutron star, the gravitational pull of the infinitely or near infinitely dense matter would result in an infinitely powerful gravitational force. The escape velocity from the infinitely powerful gravitational pull would equal the speed of light. Thus, the infinitely powerful gravitational pull would not allow anything to escape from a theoretical sphere, *the event horizon,* around the infinitely dense matter. Everything within this theoretical sphere could define what we now call a black hole.

This is the apparent reason that no form of radiation can escape from a black hole including light, X-Rays or Gamma Radiation. Further, any matter that approaches the event horizon will be drawn into the black hole without leaving any trace. Within the black hole the laws of the cosmos cease to exist, or at least they are beyond our understanding. There is no space or time. It's a point where reality ends, or perhaps where reality begins as a portal to another universe.

Then there is perhaps the greatest of all mysteries; the so-called "dark matter" and "dark energy" mysteries. We humans can only see and deal with about five percent of the mass of the universe. That five percent represents all that we can see and deal with here on Earth, and what appear to be the stars and galaxies we see in outer space and the universe. What we don't see is another 25 percent that represents what scientists call dark matter. Dark matter emits no radiation. We only know it exists, or only can guess it exists, because something is exerting what appears to be a gravitational force effecting the motion and configuration of galaxies.

The 70 percent or so of the unknown remaining is what is known in the world of physics as dark energy-matter. Dark energy-matter represents the driving force causing the expansion of the universe. We think we know that dark energy-matter exists, because if it didn't exist, galaxies and galaxy clusters could not have formed and evolved as they did, and because they would be flying apart instead of rotating in some sort of a predictable manner. As best that can be determined dark energy-matter could exist in some as yet undiscovered particle or matter. On the other hand, dark energy-matter may not exist, or it may exist in a mysterious form not yet detectable. If it doesn't exist, its absence would require a massive re-examination of our theories of physics, including Einstein's theory of relativity.

In addition to the elusiveness of dark matter and dark energy, there is as yet no law of physics linking the laws of the cosmos with the laws of quantum mechanics. String theory is an attempt to do so, but the inability to prove string theory through experimentation is likely to be a long-lived limitation. Quantum mechanics shows that matter is elusive and can be in many places at the same time. Given the elasticity of time and matter in the theory of relativity, it is not much of a stretch to conclude that matter can be recomposed and transposed in time from the past to the present, and from the present to the future, and back again, perhaps in parallel universes.

Quarks, gluons, Higgs bosons, muons and other yet to be discovered subatomic particles may be comprised of still smaller particles that exist in terms of nanoseconds. String theory is a sophisticated, yet awkward and limited approach to unifying the laws of the cosmos with quantum mechanics. Are we reaching the limits of understanding? Perhaps some new theory will allow us to conclude that our solar system is an atom, our Milky Way Galaxy a molecule, and our universe an unknown compound in a still greater unknown reality in parallel universes. Perhaps we will someday understand what came before the beginning, or to understand nothingness, or to be humbled by the concept of infinity. For now, God is hope and wonder and awe, loving our neighbors as ourselves and treating others as we would have them treat us. It's all very simple.

ABOUT THE AUTHOR

The author is a retired Registered Professional Engineer, and a retired lawyer formerly licensed in three jurisdictions and the United States Court of Appeals for the Federal Circuit. He retired from federal service as the Chief Judge of the USDA, Board of Contract Appeals (BCA). As an engineer he performed research, development and testing on gas devices for the American Gas Association, and was involved with the construction of space and rocket test facilities for the NASA's Lewis Research Center, now the John Glenn Research Center. He worked as a contracting officer for the FAA and as a lawyer for the NLRB.

The author served in the Navy Office of the General Counsel in various Naval Commands and ultimately as the Deputy Counsel for the Naval Sea Systems Command (NAVSEA); advising the Command's management hierarchy; and managing a staff of 60 attorneys nation-wide dealing with the complex legal and litigation matters resulting from the operations of NAVSEA. These operations included the acquisition of the Navy's fleet, including the Trident, Ballistic Missile Submarines, the Los Angeles Class of nuclear attack submarines, and the Nimitz Class of nuclear carriers. His clients included Admiral Hyman Rickover and the Three-Star Admirals that routinely headed NAVSEA.

As the Chief Judge of the USDA BCA, he presided over government contract disputes from all USDA agencies including the Forest Service, Soil Conservation Service, Farmers Home Administration, Food Safety and Inspection Service and the Risk Management Agency. He implemented Alternative Dispute Resolution practices to expedite appeals, reduce the costs of litigation and achieve settlements. He authored written decisions in approximately 100 appeals and served on the deciding panels in approximately 300 other appeals. BCA decisions were final within the USDA, subject to appeal to the U.S. Court of Appeals for the Federal Circuit.

In his post-retirement career the author conducted employment dispute hearings before the Fairfax Civil Service Commission; arbitrated employment and securities related disputes for the Financial Industry Regulatory Authority (FINRA); and mediated cases in contract law and patents for the U.S. Court of Appeals for the Federal Circuit; while performing pro bono legal services for Legal Services of Northern Virginia and the Fairfax Bar.

The author has had a lifelong interest in the early Christian church. He has worked in a variety of federal government positions and agencies and retired at the highest non-political level. He has witnessed the gradual usurpation of government functions and operations that have shifted the government's focus away from protecting the best interests of its citizens to protecting and promoting the best interests of the wealthy and influential exercising undue influence.